The Consciousness Cookbook

Authenticity in a Simulated Reality

Jeroen Carelse

Jeroen Carelse
jeroencarelse.com

The Consciousness Cookbook
Authenticity in a Simulated Reality

Text and illustrations: Jeroen Carelse
Fonts: Schuss Serif Pro
Published: Hattula - Jeroen Carelse, 2025

Publisher:
Jeroen Carelse
Pappilanniementie 18
13880, Hattula
Finland
jeroencarelse.com
theconsciousnesscookbook.com

ISBN 978-952-88-0056-9 (softcover)

Copyright 2025 by Jeroen Carelse

All rights reserved. This book or any portion thereof may not be reproduced or used in any manner whatsoever without the express written permission of the publisher except for the use of brief quotations in a book review.

To Leena and all those who have been with me this time around

Contents

Preface	1
Introduction	11
The Authentic Creative	14
Chapter Overview	19
Our Reality	23
The Larger Consciousness System	29
Simulations Compared	35
Consciousness is Fundamental	45
The Soul	57
Birth, Death, and Rebirth	62
The Soul's Journey	67
Collaboration, Identity, and Continuity	72
Forces	79
Good and Evil	87
Virtues and Vices	99
Shame, Blame, and Guilt	108
The Human Experience	115
Habitual Reactions and Conscious Choices	118
Choices Influenced	123
Life Paths	129
Echoes of the Infinite	137
Passive and Active Interactions	139
The Mechanics	144
The Modalities	147
Authenticity	177
Overcoming Masks and Embracing Growth	180
Tools, Techniques, and Exercises	188
Recognising progress	198
Afterword	223

Preface
Why this book and how to read it?

Since my childhood, I have had a strong desire to express my ideas freely. When life made me stay quiet, I vowed that one day I would speak my mind without reservation.

I was born on a Monday afternoon, the 25th of August 1969, in Leek, a town in the northern part of the Netherlands. I have no recollection of that first year. When I was a little over a year old, we moved to Texel, an island on the northwest coast of the Netherlands. My first memories are from that island. I remember sitting in a baby pram and hearing music coming from the radio of the milkman's vehicle.

In those early years, I had vivid memories, such as drawing an aeroplane into perspective at the age of three. My parents believed my older brothers must have drawn it, but they denied it wholeheartedly. The only explanation was that I had drawn it myself.

This early childhood experience repeated itself in various ways throughout my life. When I had done something, had seen or heard something, I was often not believed. It must have shaped me, as during my pre-teens and

Preface

early teens I had learned to keep experiences to myself. Only much later did I understand how these coping mechanisms helped me navigate social situations. What I did realise early on was that my reality, compared to that of others, could be fundamentally different. Another curious discovery I made was that information from the future, or a distant place, could enter my thought stream without me wanting or asking for it.

The period from my early to late teens was confusing. I had no clear goal and spent more time battling inner conflicts than understanding what—or who—I was truly up against. I think of those years as a steel ball ricocheting inside a pinball machine, constantly pushed in directions I didn't choose.

At the start of my industrial design studies at art school in the Netherlands, I won a prize that received significant coverage in both the national and international press. Surprisingly, the only classmate who congratulated me was a girl with whom I often had philosophical disagreements. I had expected to celebrate with my classmates, but instead, I went to town alone, called a friend from another department, and together we watched a great movie (Smoke, 1995) in a small cinema.

This experience—achieving something significant but not receiving recognition from my peers—left me confused and made me withdraw even further.

> *Recently, a professional astrologer looked at my birth chart and the decades to come. Aside from the many useful things he mentioned, one thing stood out like a sore thumb. He emphasised that "I have driven the car with the brakes on."*

Experiments and Doubts

I began writing several versions of this book more than a year ago. The first versions explored topics like quantum theory, the philosophy of science, history, and exorcism to illustrate how the body, mind, and spirit interact. After 300 pages of rich narratives, I felt drained, discouraged, and even sad. It seemed I hadn't accomplished what I set out to do: write a book that might help people. I realised that I had been writing with the goal of demonstrating my presumed intelligence. I took a break, but the pressure to act—to write—remained.

While working on the earlier versions, I experienced flashes of anxiety. Some stemmed from fears of being ridiculed, not being believed, or becoming isolated due to disbelief. These fears, though outdated, felt real. Over time, I recognised higher-level fears and traced them back to fundamental ones: abandonment, suffering, and death. These days, I have much more control over how I respond to such fears. Other doubts surfaced, like "Who would want to read this?" or "Does this book even make sense?" By investigating these questions, I uncovered an internal conflict: my desire to share my story clashed with hidden forces sowing doubt. I share this because I practise what I preach.

I may have bent a few rules while writing this book, as I wanted to do it my way. I wrote it myself, created the illustrations, and handled the layout and publishing. Thankfully, I received help with proofreading and used software to catch typos, style issues, and grammar mistakes.

I chose not to include extensive citations from research papers, other authors, or historical figures. This decision stems from my desire to avoid the distractions that often arise from debates over the validity of evidence or the superiority of one source over another. I recognise that many researchers may offer valuable insights, but they may also hold views in unrelated fields that contradict or seem outlandish. When this happens, readers can become fixated on those contradictions, overlooking the more relevant and coherent arguments in favour of minor discrepancies. I want to avoid this tendency, as it can shift focus away from the core message I aim to convey.

Instead, I want you, the reader, to engage directly with my reasoning. I believe that intellectual engagement should be personal and self-reliant, and that, by focusing on my logic, I can encourage you to think critically and form your own conclusions. The strength of my arguments lies not in external validation, but in their internal consistency and the clarity of their structure. This approach aligns with the broader themes of authenticity and self-reliance that I explore throughout this book.

By not relying on citations, I also hope to nurture a deeper connection with you, the reader. I want you to engage with these ideas on your own terms, without being swayed by the opinions or authority of others. This is not to say that other perspectives do not exist, but rather that the exploration of these ideas should be an open and personal process. I encourage you to look inward, to search for logic and understanding within yourself, and to embrace a more authentic form of intellectual engagement. In this way, I hope this book serves as a catalyst for deeper reflection, self-awareness, and personal growth.

In addition to the above cautions, writing a book like this on among other metaphysics, philosophy and esoteric concepts gives ample room to construct carefully crafted texts, that consider all possible views, logic, and illogic on a given subject. I have tried to avoid a language that would make me sound more like a legal counsellor than a curious explorer of Consciousness. So yes, I admit, at times I shoot from the hip and let my intuitive-knowing speak rather than the pondering, careful and deliberate other side.

The Authentic Me
In the chapters ahead, I attempt to organise my notes, structure my thoughts, formalise my findings, and provide real-life examples. I use the word "attempt" intentionally, as my thinking tends to examine topics from multiple angles. Presenting every nuance and counterargument would make the book unreadable and overly long. For example, there are many Simulation Theories. While I could delve into the intricacies of each, doing so would require several chapters, not just a sentence. At times, I may express my views confidently, but please remember that other perspectives and nuances exist. I fully acknowledge this.

This book tells a story—my story—of how I perceive and experience reality. It is deeply personal, and I hope the emotions conveyed resonate with you. Writing these experiences helps me reflect on my progress and recognise how many past emotions no longer surface, though some still do. I hope these experiences serve as a mirror, offering encouragement and hope. I also hope you understand the logic I describe and try some suggestions to gain more control over your life.

This book reflects my experimental nature. As I reviewed the chapters, I recognised remnants of earlier versions. Initially, it was a simple handout for students based on workshop topics. Later, I envisioned a concise 60-page pocket guide, which explains the abrupt, "chop chop chop" sentences in some parts. Before that, it was a sprawling 300-page philosophical exploration. At one point, I even imagined it as a richly illustrated children's book, but doubts about my illustration skills held me back. For a time, I called it The Consciousness Cookbook, enjoying the idea of outlining concepts as recipes for understanding Consciousness. That working title eventually became the final title.

> *I write throughout this book Consciousness with a capital C when I mean Consciousness as the fundamental essence that makes up reality.*
>
> *In contemporary psychology and neuroscience, "consciousness" (lowercase) refers to the brain's measurable activity and processes, such as conscious awareness of thoughts or perceptions, whereas "Consciousness" (uppercase) denotes a philosophical or metaphysical concept of an underlying, fundamental reality beyond empirical neural correlates.*
>
> *I write it in lowercase. I prefer to use the words "conscious awareness" when referring to mental processes, such as registering a thought.*

Style

I chose not to homogenise the writing style, not out of neglect but as a consciously aware decision. Homogenising the writing style would have taken another year,[1] and I wanted to release the book. This reflects my priorities and personality—I learn by doing and experimenting, taking risks, not by strictly adhering to a guidebook on how to write a book.

This will not be "the perfect book", and I do not mind. I already experienced during the editing phases that I can add other angels and insights, remove oblique phrases and improve the illustrations. Yes, all is true, but at the same time, I need to draw a line somewhere. I can draw new lines in an updated version, or in a new book.

This book defies categorisation. It blends ideas, styles, and perspectives, all carefully considered after years of study, reflection, and experimentation. It is not "just a book" but a potentially valuable exploration of simulation theory and Tom Campbell's Larger Consciousness System. Not only that, but it also offers practical, no-cost techniques to navigate life more effectively. In its imperfection lies its authenticity, and in its authenticity, I hope you find value.

Authenticity

In this book, I frequently use the term "authentic," and it's important to clear up a common misconception right from the start. When I mention authenticity, I'm referring to the alignment of consciously aware thoughts, words, and actions with your Soul (defined in later chapters) —an entity that holds your core qualities and the original intentions you had for being in this simulation. The Soul isn't fixed in quality; it can evolve and devolve over time, shaped by the choices and actions you make within the simulation.

It's essential to understand that authenticity doesn't necessarily mean being "enlightened," "holy," or "good" in the conventional sense. One can be authentic even if their Soul is of low quality, as long as their actions reflect that low quality. In this way, someone who acts out of greed, lust, or fear may still be authentic, but that doesn't make them a good person. Authenticity simply means alignment with the Soul's current state, whether that state is one of higher or lower entropy.

To put this bluntly: one can be truly rotten, authentically rotten.

Higher entropy represents chaos, disorder, and actions driven by fear or selfishness, while lower entropy reflects love, collaboration, and the creation of positive outcomes. As a Soul moves through the simulation, it can either grow toward lower entropy, leading to greater harmony and a more meaningful existence. Or the Soul moves toward higher entropy, where it becomes less valuable to the Larger Consciousness System (LCS) and may eventually lose its identity.

The key to growth, whether towards higher or lower entropy, lies in how the Soul responds to the influences within the simulation—such as upbringing, education, and the actions of others—while exercising its free will. These influences shape the unconscious patterns that guide the Soul's choices. Overcoming these patterns requires effort and practice, often involving both introspection and feedback from others. While the process can be challenging, with time and conscious effort, it becomes easier, as the Soul integrates its true intentions into everyday life.

Love and Fear

Tom uses typically the words love and fear, and I use those too in this book. But I have decided to interchange these words with synonyms and words that work better in certain context. Another reason is that whatever word I would have decided to use, that word would be understood differently by different audiences. So by using a wider variety of words, you, the reader, stay alert and get to sense the broader meaning of Tom's core concepts.

Love	Fear
Low entropy	High entropy
Order	Chaos
Good	Evil
Light	Darkness

Definitions and flow

Aside from the various labels I use for love and fear, I also create my meanings for words such as authenticity, Soul, Self, and you. These, and many other words, are so common and have acquired so many meanings that they have become nearly meaningless. The challenge I encountered while writing this book was finding the right moment to introduce a word like "authentic" and deciding when to present my definition of it.

My first objective was to ensure logical chapter flow, achieved by progressing from explaining the Larger Consciousness System (which governs real-life forces) to methods for balancing these forces, and finally to measuring success in such efforts.

The next priority has been to create a logical flow within each chapter. This proved to be a tougher challenge, as nearly every sentence or paragraph opened more than one possible direction. For example, when faced with multiple options, such as whether to explain a newly introduced concept in detail immediately or later, I decided to interject the text flow with definitions that support my thesis, such as authenticity, Soul, and you. In other cases, I described the concepts within the text in various forms throughout the book. As a result, you will encounter repetition, most of which has been deliberate.

Tom Campbell

I do not know Tom, he politely answered some of my emails, and those answers were succinct and to the point. I appreciate that. I got his book on my shelf and started reading the first of three parts (it is a trilogy) but never got to part two and three. Instead, I did watch and listened to his videos, especially those workshop videos which have many parts and cover many hours. I seem to get more out of watching him speak than reading the printed words. That is just me and if you are a book reader I encourage you to start reading his book. I am convinced it is full of interesting bits and bobs.

It might have been a bit over ten years ago that I got to listen to one of Tom's videos. Some time before 2015 for sure, maybe 2012, possibly 2014. I am not good with remembering dates as I don't find it intriguing. I mention the approximate year of first contact because it took me some years before his model made sense on a "being level" and not only as an intellectual pursuit. I mention this for two reasons.

The first reason is my increased patience in explaining the LCS—understanding requires time for intellectual-logical grasp and experiential integration through experimentation, testing, and note-taking; comprehension hinges on lived experience, not belief (though belief may initiate the journey).

The second reason to mention the approximate first time I encountered Tom's theory is that, some years ago, I was contacted by email by a French documentary maker. He sent a short and polite email thanking me for outlining Tom's theory on my (now removed) website. He finally "got it" he wrote. I am paraphrasing as I lost the email. The point here is that although Tom's theory is solid, and he explains in great detail the logic and intricacies, some people need a slightly or radically different approach. I wrote the outline to make it clear to myself and other people appreciated this.

This experience about the need for experience and the email are fundamental to me writing this book. I propose a few tools to experiment with, tools to test your progress, and I describe Tom's theory differently to his. Although I, of course, try to stay as close as possible to his concept. Still, pick up his book, watch his videos and above all: try.

Introduction
The Soul's Journey in a Simulated Reality

In this book, I share ideas from physicist and Consciousness researcher Tom Campbell. He talks about his Simulation Theory and the Larger Consciousness System (LCS). Tom wrote a trilogy called My Big TOE, which stands for My Big Theory of Everything. He combines physics, Consciousness, and metaphysics to help us understand the bigger picture of reality. But he goes further, looking beyond the physical to include non-physical aspects. "My" emphasises that this isn't about strict beliefs; it's about personal exploration. He encourages you not to take someone else's truth at face value. Instead, explore for yourself. Your journey might lead you to your truth or TOE.

> *Consciousness*
> *Tom describes Consciousness as awareness with a Will. This Consciousness also needs memory, a place to store the experiences, and logic. The logic is I would describe as coherency and consistency combined with causality. So if one thing happens once under specific circumstances, the same thing under the same circumstances should happen again. One could write books about the nature of Consciousness, but that for someone else or for some other time.*

Introduction

Believing something too firmly can hinder your growth. To truly grow, you should seek where your beliefs have come from, and work on understanding the role they play in your life. You need to seek who you are and what you want in life to grow. Tom's trilogy explores how he reached his ideas, and his later videos and presentations not only give more details, but also show his growth as he adds more insights to his original ideas. I won't try to sum up his work or his videos on LCS and Simulation Theory. But I'll give you a simple overview of what the LCS means, based on what I've learned.

Simulation Theory, in this context, suggests our reality functions like a simulation. Not that we're actually inside a computer, but as a metaphor to explain how we experience life. Imagine it as a hyperrealistic video game. You might feel immersed in that world, but it consists solely of information and code. In this view, your Soul is like the player in this game I call "Life on Earth."

Another example of experiencing a "simulation" is when you read a book or watch a movie. You might have felt deeply connected to a character in a movie or a book. After some watching or reading, you begin to "feel" what one or more characters feel. The movie or book gradually has become part of your reality. Life on Earth is as if you are in a play. From when you started sensing things around you, inside your mother's womb, you stepped into a convincing show. By the time you know who you are, your senses convince you this is all there is.

When you were young, you might have had some memories of what it was before you came here. However, those fade away quickly, like waking up from a dream. There is a good reason why you won't remember much and why these memories fade away so quickly. And when you have been "alive" for a while, it's all about learning how to survive and manage in this "Life on Earth."

As you interact with the world, you face choices. Those choices lead to growth or decline, love or fear, order or chaos. Your Soul plays this game repeatedly, focusing on different lessons each time. To learn effectively, you retain your core qualities but not memories from past lives.

The Soul Soup

When I say Soul, I'm talking about that part of you that never goes away. It's the part you might sense during a Near-Death Experience, or NDE. When I say "you," I mean the part of you playing the "Life on Earth" game. You and your Soul are connected but different.

Your Soul knows everything about you, but has a hard time communicating with you. You have little understanding of your Soul, and you can't distinguish between the chatter in your mind and your Soul talking to you. Occasionally, I'll use the term "Self" to mean "you and your Soul" together. I'll aim to write it out completely, but I might not stick to that all the time.

The Authentic Creative
Theoretical Integration of Samsara, the Three-Body Problem, and the Larger Consciousness System

In my way of thinking, I often find myself drawn to symbols and concepts not for their literal meaning, but for the possibilities they represent. I am at times a symbolic thinker, someone who takes familiar symbols—whether they are cultural, linguistic, or scientific—and sees them as starting points for new ideas, theories, and understanding. I don't just accept a symbol's conventional meaning; I explore how it connects to other ideas, how it might evolve in a different context, or what new interpretations might emerge when viewed in a new light. This desire to see beyond the surface allows me to build conceptual bridges between seemingly unrelated fields or to explore abstract possibilities that, I hope, will open doors to new ideas.

This process is not about discarding the original meanings of symbols but expanding their potential. I use what is already known as a foundation, but I am constantly investigating how to push beyond this, to apply it in ways that challenge conventional thinking. For example, where others might see a symbol as static or fixed, I see it as a dynamic tool, an evolving entity, capable of revealing new insights. Whether I am exploring metaphors in literature, concepts in science, or even everyday objects, I consistently seek to reframe them. I ask "What if?" and imagine how these symbols could contribute to a new theory or understanding of the world. At one moment the idea came to mind that Samsara, the Three Body Problem and the LCS could be used to visualise the core dynamics of Life on Earth:

There are forces that push and pull at us, we are a force too. When we use our force consciously and with the right intent, we can create a more deliberate life.

Samsara

Samsara is a key idea in Buddhism. It means the never-ending cycle of being born, dying, and being born again. See it as a journey where your Soul experiences many lives. Each life helps us learn and grow.

In each lifetime, we face challenges and opportunities. These challenges help you to let go of ignorance (to lower entropy) and get closer to your authentic Self. The goal isn't just to break free from this cycle. It's about becoming more aware and understanding things better.

By authentically engaging with life, you change the quality of your Soul. It's all about learning and evolving through our experiences. Reincarnation isn't just a repeat cycle. It's a chance for deep growth. Each life is potentially a step toward being more authentic, as the Soul learns from your choices and intentions.

Three-Body Problem

The Three-Body Problem is a way to describe how three things in space move because of gravity and the interaction between those gravitational forces creates unpredictability: chaos. I use the metaphor to illustrate how life as we experience it feels chaotic out outside our control.

I propose we have three main forces at play in our lives: chaos (evil), order (love), and Self. Self is a combination of You and your Soul. My theory suggests that when You and your Soul have become one, which I call being authentic, the Three-Body Problem is solved. You are then the stabilising body.

When you understand and accept these different forces, you have a chance to grow as a person, and not be at the mercy of those "invisible" forces. After recognition and acceptance, you begin the journey towards authenticity. You start to feel more real and true to yourself.

In my thinking, those three bodies are chaos, order, and our conscious awareness (you). Tom Campbell's system encapsulates the cycle of rebirth (Samsara) and the complex dynamics of chaos and order (fear and love) where you play a decisive role. Your Soul grows or degrades through experiencing many lives in simulations like Life on Earth. The aim is to bring down chaos and find love and order. The reason is that chaos in any system results in the collapse of that system. Thus, the Larger Consciousness System benefits from less chaos, and your Soul benefits from less chaos. I get back to this concept in a later chapter.

Each person is like a unique piece of Consciousness. You're separate from, and also linked to your Soul. You, as a conscious being, live within life's simulation but stay connected to your Soul through for example intuitions, dreams and strange experiences. Connecting the "you" with the Soul is very beneficial for growth.

The Three-Body Problem metaphor is used to illustrate the interaction between three forces:

> *Chaos (lots of disorder) pushes and pulls at us, often bringing fear and negativity.*
> *Order (more stability) also pushes and pulls, showing love and goodness.*
> *You (your conscious awareness) and soul, which try to balance these forces.*

Good and evil, love and fear, are part of chaos and order. They shape how we think, act, and choose. While being inside this simulation, we can learn to understand the forces at play, and find a balance between chaotic and orderly elements within those forces. But achieving this balance isn't easy on Earth. We face constant challenges and distractions.

Becoming authentic is an ongoing process. It needs both looking within ourselves and taking actions that let our conscious awareness and Soul work together. When they are aligned, we can handle life's chaos and order better. If our Soul isn't fully integrated, we might feel lost amid chaos. A fully integrated Soul is I think a goal, and you will have achieved it when you don't need to return to this simulation for further learning the specific lessons this simulation offers.

Thus, reincarnation is key here. It lets the Soul evolve by living many different lives and facing a wide variety of challenges. Each life is a chance to learn, confront chaos and lower our entropy, and refine our understanding of love, fear, good, and evil. With each life, you and your Soul can make better choices, moving closer to love and order.

The Influence of Negative Thoughts and Fear on Decision-Making and the Transition to the Soul

The Three-Body Problem and Samsara are sources of inspiration for me; I do not feel the urge to defend them or integrate them scholarly in my thesis. What I find inspiring is that this thinking illustrates how your path towards becoming authentic, stabilises the otherwise seemingly chaotic pushing and pulling of those "good and evil" forces.

One main point I like to get across is that the perceived opposites of Evil and Good are not as black and white as often presented. I see those polarities more as magnetic opposites with a force field in between. That these polarities exist and have real effect I do not deny nor downplay.

In this book, I define both as clear opposites, but also show the wide spectrum that bridges both. And I present many cases where aspects of "Evil" can be productive, and where aspects of "Good" can be counterproductive. I try to avoid blindly embracing existing philosophies, theories or dogmas, and instead build from the ground up my theory based on observation, ratio, and intuition.

Introduction

In this book, I extensively dissect the Catholic dogma of the Seven Sins and Virtues, and a more modern perspective on personal and social forces in the form of shame, blame, guilt and such. I consider especially feelings of shame, guilt and blaming others are external forces that can be beneficial or destructive.

The forces of chaos (high entropy) and order (low entropy) shape the decisions we make throughout our lives, often in ways we are not fully aware of. Negative thoughts, rooted in fear, can have a profound influence on our decision-making process. Fear, as an intrinsic part of chaos, can pull individuals toward extremes—whether it be the extreme of lust or the extreme of chastity.

Lust, for example, can be driven by a fear of inadequacy, the fear of not being desired or loved, leading individuals to seek external validation through physical or superficial connections. This fear of rejection or loneliness can fuel a compulsive pursuit of pleasure, often disconnected from deeper emotional or spiritual fulfilment.

On the other hand, chastity, when driven by fear, can manifest as an extreme form of self-denial, rooted in shame or guilt about one's desires. The fear here is often the fear of judgment, the fear of being considered immoral or unworthy. Individuals may suppress their natural urges, believing that abstinence or self-control is the only path to virtue, but this suppression can be just as fear-driven as the indulgence in lust. The fear of being "too human" or "too weak" can lead to a rigid, emotionally disconnected way of living, where one's natural desires are repressed rather than integrated.

In this way, both extremes—lust and chastity—are fuelled by underlying fears, but they manifest in different ways. The fear of death, and the negative thoughts associated with it, can profoundly affect not only how we live but also how we experience the transition from life to death. Fear of death can cloud the transition, creating a more chaotic and unsettling experience. This fear may be rooted in misconceptions or cultural constructs that reinforce the idea of death as an end rather than a return to the Soul. The more fear is allowed to dominate, the more chaotic the experience of dying can become. On the other hand, a life lived with alignment with the Soul, where love and order have been prioritised over fear, can ease the transition, allowing the individual to return to the Soul with greater peace and acceptance.

Chapter Overview

Chapter 1: Our Reality
I compare two views of reality: Physicalism, which focuses on matter and biological processes, and Idealism, which sees Consciousness as fundamental. I share how Tom's Larger Consciousness System (LCS) explains reality as a simulation, where Souls grow through choices and experiences. I also use relatable examples, like video games, to explain how this simulation works and why it's designed the way it is.

> *1.1 The Larger Consciousness System*
> The LCS is introduced as a framework where Consciousness evolves through collaboration, complexity, and simulations. Souls emerge as individuated units of Consciousness, learning and growing through structured experiences.
>
> *1.2 Simulations Compared*
> The chapter explores different simulations, such as "Life on Earth," dreams, remote viewing, and near-death experiences, highlighting their unique rules and purposes while showing their interconnectedness.

Chapter 2: The Soul
I explore what the Soul is and its journey through life, death, and rebirth. The Soul retains its core qualities across lifetimes but wipes memories to allow for fresh learning experiences. I discuss how the Soul collaborates with others, maintains its identity, and evolves through continuity across lives.

> *2.1 Birth, Death, and Rebirth*
> The transition between lives is explained, focusing on how the Soul sheds old identities while carrying forward its essence.
>
> *2.2 The Soul's Journey*
> Challenges and opportunities for growth are presented as the central purpose of the Soul's experiences across lifetimes.
>
> *2.3 Collaboration, Identity, and Continuity*
> The interactions of the Soul with others, its development of identity, and its ability to maintain continuity in its broader journey are discussed.

Chapter 3: Forces
This chapter explores the forces of love and fear, order and chaos, good and evil. I discuss how these forces shape our choices and growth. Fear is broken down into levels, from basic survival instincts to deeper, more complex fears like shame and guilt. I show how these emotions can either block or support growth, depending on how we handle them.

> ### 3.1 Good and Evil
> The nature of good and evil is explored as a spectrum rather than a strict dichotomy, with actions and intentions shaping outcomes.
>
> ### 3.2 Virtues and Vices
> Traits that help or hinder growth are examined, showing how they connect to the forces of love and fear.
>
> ### 3.3 Shame, Blame, and Guilt
> The impact of these emotions on choices is discussed, along with how they can be transformed into tools for personal growth.

Chapter 4: The Human Experience
I explore how our habits, choices, and life paths shape our growth. I talk about three main paths: the authentic path, the shortcut path, and the corruption path. Each reflects different ways we handle life's challenges and influences.

> ### 4.1 Habitual Reactions and Conscious Choices
> The patterns and automatic responses that shape our lives are explored, highlighting the role of conscious choice.
>
> ### 4.2 Choices Influenced
> External factors and internal fears are examined for their impact on decision-making.
>
> ### 4.3 Life Paths
> The three life paths are outlined, showing how they influence personal growth and alignment with the Soul.

Chapter 5: Echoes of the Infinite
This chapter focuses on how we connect with the Larger Consciousness System (LCS). I introduce tools like meditation, journaling, and remote viewing to help you engage with the LCS and measure progress.

5.1 Passive and Active Interactions
The differences between observing and actively engaging with the LCS are explained.

5.2 The Mechanics
Practical aspects of connecting with the LCS are discussed, including how these interactions work.

5.3 The Modalities
Specific techniques and exercises for engaging with the LCS are presented, offering flexible methods for different goals.

Chapter 6: Authenticity

I share my personal journey toward authenticity, exploring how alignment with the Soul leads to growth. I elaborate on the masks we wear, the societal pressures we face, and the tools we can use to measure progress.

6.1 Overcoming Masks and Embracing Growth
The barriers to authenticity are identified, along with ways to confront and overcome them.

6.2 Tools, Techniques, and Exercises
Practical methods for evaluating progress and aligning with your true Self are provided.

6.3 Recognising Progress
Ways to track personal growth and maintain authenticity are highlighted.

Afterword

I conclude by reflecting on the journey this book represents. It's not about achieving perfection but about understanding and aligning with your Soul's current state.

I advocate for gradual and manageable steps to personal growth, emphasising the importance of trust, creativity, and judgment in navigating life. Techniques for evaluating progress, such as writing letters to one's future self, using astrology, reflecting on dreams, and analysing personal relationships, are proposed as tools for developing authenticity and understanding one's journey. The text also touches on the significance of learning from regrets and near-death experiences, summarising that the essence of living authentically is about being true to oneself, rather than conforming to external expectations.

1
Our Reality
Where Idealism Includes Physicalism

Like most of mine, and later generations, I grew up with the narrative that our reality is made from atoms (stuff). I still remember the white and red plastic spheres in chemistry classes that symbolise what our reality is made of. The story is that our reality is made of off stuff, and mental processes are a result of chemical and electromagnetic interactions between all kinds of stuff. Feelings of love, sadness, or the taste of chocolate are because of these interactions. For a long time, this thinking about reality made perfect sense to me, as much can be explained with this thinking. I got older and encountered phenomena that I was unable to explain or had experiences that I could not explain with the theory of stuff. That these phenomena and experiences were coincidences, imagination, or nonsense did not cut for me any more.

However, from a very early age, I seem to have known about molecules and the principle of matter and that it played an important role in what I experienced.

> *My parents often reminded me of a car trip when I was young. I was probably around 3 years old. All I can recall is looking out the window as we drove through the Netherlands, smelling something like cow dung. I distinctly remember saying, 'I smell cow-shit molecules', using the word "shit" instead of 'manure'. I didn't learn about the connection between gases and molecules from my family. However, since my father worked in the chemical industry, I may have subconsciously absorbed some of his knowledge. I will not explore the concept of telepathy in this book.*

So it is not that I think Physicalism has no place, and should be replaced. I think Physicalism is very valuable, and we need to keep on investigating, so to find yet undiscovered principles to explain our physical reality. Having that said, I now consider Physicalism a subset of something larger. In other words, something larger encompasses Physicalism, and does not replace it.

A most compressed overview ever
To keep things simply, I consider only the two main world views: Physicalism, which holds that everything is made up of matter, and a Consciousness-based view, suggesting that our world is part of a larger, non-material reality. This Consciousness based reality, not to be mistaken for conscious awareness as used in modern psychology, I call Idealism at times. And thus we have Physicalism and Idealism as the two main world views. I shall spend very little time on talking about Physicalism, as the bookshelves are already filled with enough explanations about that worldview.

But let me, in a brutal manner, summarise the main differences in this way. Physicalism sees life as limited to e.g. electromagnetic, chemical, and biological processes. These processes give rise to your awareness, your will, your thoughts, and emotions. When these processes falter, diseases might occur, and when the body stops working altogether, it is game over and nothing is left of you. This thinking results in the belief that you got one chance to make the best of it, eventually resulting in a focus on material possessions and scepticism toward the unseen. Related are the monotheistic religions, which more or less tell you there is one lifetime, make the best of it. In contrast, Idealism (a Consciousness-centric worldview akin to Eastern belief systems) frames life as the Soul's multi-lifetime journey, where virtues like kindness and patience refine or diminish its essence. This book is about how Consciousness is fundamental to our reality and experiences, and how to influence your direction in life.

Early humans believed everything in nature was alive, naturally connecting with unseen forces, through shamans and rituals. Later societies added the worship of many gods, using myths to explain natural events and their origins. Greek philosophy shifted thought toward reason and observation, laying the foundations for scientific inquiry. In the Middle Ages, Monotheism such as Christianity focused on life as a path to either heaven or hell, until the Renaissance introduced humanism, celebrating human creativity and achievement.

The Enlightenment emphasised reason, individual rights, and observation, leading to new scientific advances and a view of the universe as orderly and predictable. The idea about the Soul became more or less the exclusive domain of "the church". And gradually the mind became the domain of materialistic thinking. Romanticism reacted to this rationalism, encouraging a deeper connection to emotion and nature. Later, the Industrial Revolution reinforced materialism, prioritising tangible progress and technological gains.

In the 20th century, quantum theory and Consciousness studies began to challenge traditional materialist ideas, suggesting that reality might be less predictable and that Consciousness itself could play a fundamental role in our existence. Today, Physicalism remains the leading view in the industrialised world, yet interest in the Consciousness-based model is steadily growing. This model offers a new understanding of reality, one that encourages a more compassionate and connected view of life.

Introducing Tom's thinking

When we consider this Consciousness-based view more closely, we look at Tom's Larger Consciousness System (LCS), a model that describes reality as a kind of simulation where Souls interact, evolve, and develop through choices and experiences. The LCS links with ideas from Quantum Theory, Information Theory and Simulation Theory to explain the nature of existence and how Consciousness functions. In this framework, Consciousness is not just an abstract idea but part of an active system where every experience, relationship, and decision contribute to the growth (or decline) of our Soul within a larger simulated reality.

Within the LCS, the previously discovered physical laws remain valid and useful; Physicalism. Consider the LCS as an envelope around physical reality, extending what we already know and can work with. I have noticed that too many people view the reality described by classical physics – physical reality, if you will – as being in opposition to simulation theory. This is, I think, one of the problems with contemporary science: a deliberate or at least misplaced misunderstanding of simulation theory.

At some point, the current scientific method excluded phenomena that could not be reproduced, falsified or observed empirically. This would limit the very useful scientific method of systematic process of observation, hypothesis formulation, experimentation, and analysis to understand and explain natural phenomena. Natural phenomena except those that are labelled para-normal, metaphysical or spiritual.

> ... It (scientific method) is based on materialism, which is defined (by) the theory that physical matters are **the only reality** and that all being in processes and phenomena can be explained as the manifestations or results of matter.
>
> Ingo Swann 2006,
lecture International RV Association

Simulation example

Imagine you're playing a computer game like Call of Duty, a first-person shooter game where players control all kinds of characters in various missions. In this game, your character–and you– gain new abilities and skills over time, much like how you develop skills and experiences throughout your life. You can customise your character's appearance and change roles before you start a "life", or game. But, when you first start playing this game, you get the basic outfit and gear, and gadgets. During the playing of many games you begin to collect skills, outfits, gear and experience. Over time, you can choose what kind of fighter you enjoy playing, for instance a sniper, which has specific gear and gadgets and qualities. In another game, you might want to play a helicopter pilot.

Life on Earth, within this analogy, is one of the more challenging game simulations. The lifespan is short, mirroring quick game sessions that require rapid skill acquisition and adaptation. The game on Earth emphasises the need for necessities like food and materials for shelter are essential for survival. However, the challenge intensifies, as some characters become greedy, seeking more than their basic needs, much like players who prioritise accumulating resources over genuine personal growth. This greed leads to competition and inequality, similar to characters spawning in hostile or disadvantaged zones within the game, where some players face greater obstacles than others.

Additionally, free will in the game allows you to make choices that shape your character's path, reflecting free will in real life. You can decide to help others, compete fiercely, or pursue personal goals, each choice leading to different outcomes. Personal growth varies, as not all characters develop at the same rate, mirroring the varied trajectories of human development across different regions.

When your character is eliminated in the game, the game restarts for that character, but you, the player, remain unaffected:alive. Each time you play, you bring the experiences and lessons learned from previous games, just as you carry forward knowledge and insights from experiences in life. This process mirrors the concepts of life, death, and rebirth. In this analogy, the character represents your current life, while you—the player—symbolise the Soul. When the character (life) ends, the Soul persists, carrying forward the knowledge and experiences gained to the next incarnation (new game).

Importantly, the game programme generates a new character each time the player decides to continue playing. There are no dormant characters stored on your hard drive or in the cloud, nor are there dead characters left on the battlefield indefinitely. Instead, once a character is eliminated, it remains on the battlefield briefly as a testament to that particular life experience before being cleared away. This is similar to how memories and lessons from past lives remain with those who are left behind, but gradually fade. The programme creates a fresh character whenever you, the player (Soul), choose to start another round of the game (life). As you continue to play, you accumulate more experience, earn more points, and develop greater skills and insights into how to learn and grow, paralleling personal growth and the acquisition of wisdom over multiple lifetimes.

Courageous participation

True learning doesn't happen when you're hiding in a corner. It happens through active participation and making choices amidst interactions. Similarly, in the game, you gain valuable experience by engaging directly with the game environment and other players, rather than solely relying on reading the manual, watching others play, or practising in demo modes. In real life, while reading books, listening to mentors, and attending workshops are beneficial, genuine learning and personal growth occur when you engage with real people and navigate real-life situations. Just as interacting with other players and facing challenges in the game enhances your skills, building relationships and overcoming obstacles in life encourages true development.

This analogy highlights how life can be thought of as a dynamic game simulation, where each person functions as a character guided by the Soul. You develop skills, explore various paths, and face challenges that shape your growth—much like a game character acquires abilities, transitions between roles, and confronts difficulties.

When the character's game comes to an end, the player remains and can begin another game. You carry the experiences and lessons gained onto future adventures. Your Soul continues to exist beyond a single lifetime, accumulating wisdom through multiple lives. The analogy illustrates that authentic learning and growth arise from actively working with the world and others, rather than observing passively. By fully participating and making intentional choices in life's game, you evolve, adapt, and move closer to greater understanding and purpose.

I get to the origins and logic of various simulations next in this book.

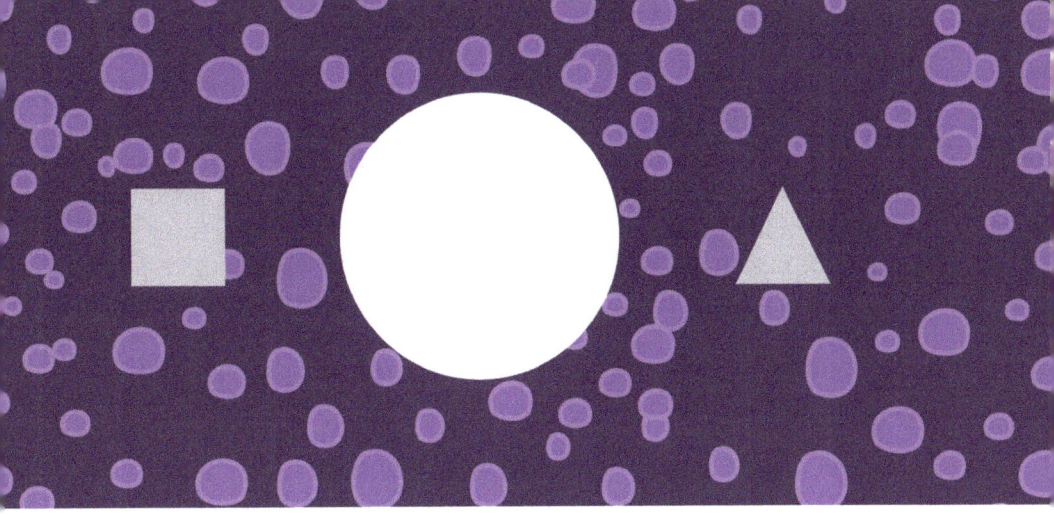

1.1

The Larger Consciousness System

The Framework Behind Life's Meaning and Our Role in It

Tom Campbell's book "My Big TOE" explores the idea that our reality is rooted in Consciousness, with love as a central tenet. Physics enters the picture through the concept of entropy. In the LCS model, Consciousness serves as the foundation of reality, rather than just a result of brain activity. It comprises a vast network of interconnected Individuated Units of Consciousness (IUoC). The LCS, or Larger Consciousness System, is a system for implementing the idea that all things originate from Consciousness. It structures how fundamental Consciousness evolves and interacts, promoting growth and development.

> *I regard Consciousness as fundamental. I regard matter as derivative from Consciousness. We cannot get behind Consciousness. Everything that we talk about, everything that we regard as existing, postulates Consciousness.*
>
> Max Planck,
25 Jan 1931,
Sun The Observer

Explaining the Larger Consciousness System (LCS) is a tricky task. Words like "Consciousness", "data", or "information" carry meanings from psychology, technology, religion, and New Age beliefs. In this context, "Consciousness" doesn't mean what it does in everyday psychology. It's something far more expansive. To avoid confusion, I'll start with the simplest definition of Consciousness and build from there, step by step, into the reality you're experiencing right now as you read these words.

Along the way, I'll touch on ideas that might feel like "magic" or mystery. That's because we're dealing with concepts that go beyond our everyday understanding. For example, I'll take it as a given that Consciousness is aware and has a will. Trying to explain *why* Consciousness is aware or *how* it has a will would open a philosophical can of worms. Instead, I'll focus on how these qualities lead to the world we know.

The story I'm about to tell is just that—a story. It's a logical one, but it's also compressed. To follow it, you'll need to sit back, read with an open mind, and let the ideas unfold. My goal is to show you how Consciousness and Souls might have come into existence, and how the world we experience is a natural result of Consciousness trying to understand itself.

The Logic of Consciousness

Consciousness: Awareness with a Will

The simplest definition: Consciousness is awareness with a will. It's aware of itself, observes its thoughts, and reflects on its actions. Its will allows it to direct attention toward a goal and, when possible, take action.

Imagine a mental void where nothing happens. You're just observing, aware that you're observing. At some point, you notice that you can direct your attention—either toward the surrounding nothingness or toward your reflection on that nothingness. This is how you discover your will. You can now choose to observe or reflect.

The Problem with Nothingness
At this stage, existence is almost meaningless—and frankly, boring. Consciousness has a will, and it quickly realises that doing nothing isn't just dull; it's deeply unsatisfying. To survive and grow, Consciousness needs stimulation. But since there's nothing else around, it has to create that stimulation itself.

Consciousness begins to play with thoughts, observing how it reacts to them. Some thoughts are coherent and lead somewhere; others are random and go nowhere. Over time, Consciousness realises that to get anywhere meaningful, it requires more coherence, more order—what we might call lower entropy.

The Birth of Souls
After a while, Consciousness creates coherent narratives and ideas. But it soon hits a wall: thinking alone has limits. It keeps repeating the same thoughts, stuck in a loop of reflecting on nothingness. To break free, Consciousness wonders: *What if I create more like myself?* And so, it creates smaller versions of itself—little awarenesses with their wills. Let's call these Souls.

Richer Interactions
Now, Consciousness isn't alone. It observes and reflects on the thoughts and actions of these Souls. At first, the Souls simply reflect on the 'nothingness' around them. But soon, they become aware of each other and start reacting to one another's thoughts. Some thoughts lead nowhere, while others spark more refined and defined ideas.

Consciousness realises that disjointed thoughts create chaos and noise, which don't lead to anything meaningful. Too much chaos, and the community of Souls becomes nothing more than noise in the void.

Collaboration and Complexity
Consciousness observes that thoughts alone have limitations. They either lead to chaos or to coherent ideas. Coherent thoughts emerge when multiple Souls build on each other's ideas logically. This collaboration leads to more complex thoughts, which eventually evolve into stories.

Souls notice that by contributing to each other's thoughts, something larger than themselves emerges. But to keep track of these complex thoughts, they need memory. Souls and

Consciousness need to remember the earlier stages of a thought to build on it.

Beyond Thought: The Need for Something Tangible
At some point, Consciousness, and the Souls ask: *What if we can expand beyond thoughts?* They imagine other forms of input and output—something beyond just thinking. They realise that for consequences to emerge, there needs to be something created that stays. This something can't be discarded at will; it must persist so that others can observe and build on it.

This idea is fundamental to the Larger Consciousness System. When something is created, it can't be removed. And when something else is added, time is created. Time is about before and after: first there was this, then there was that. Similarly, space emerges when something takes up a place beyond nothingness.

The First Objects and the Emergence of Chaos
The first non-thought object is created and observed. Consciousness has added an input channel (awareness of the object) and an output channel (the creation of the object). But here's the catch: once one Soul creates an object, the others can only add to it. This limits their choices and leads to chaos as random objects clutter the void.

The Need for Sandboxes
To solve this, Consciousness creates insulated environments—sandboxes—where Souls can experiment without interfering with each other. Some Souls keep their sandboxes private, while others invite fellow Souls to collaborate. This introduces the concepts of "mine" and "yours."

The Evolution of Souls
Over time, Souls develop different preferences and traits. Some enjoy building alone, while others thrive in groups. These differences mark the beginnings of emotions, character traits, and identity. Consciousness itself evolves, enriched by the variety of input and output from its Souls.

Simulations with Rules
To manage the growing complexity, Consciousness creates simulations with specific rules. In some simulations, objects can't be removed once created. In others, removal is allowed under certain conditions. These rulesets become increasingly

intricate, leading to stable environments like solar systems and planets.

Vessels for Souls
In these physical simulations, Souls need vessels—bodies—to experience the world. These bodies allow Souls to see, hear, feel, and taste their environment. We label those as our five senses. The bodies are prone to damage and destruction. Survival becomes a priority, and Souls learn from each other, and from interacting with the environment.

Body, Mind and Soul
During the early phase of life in this physical simulation, the Soul is fully dependent on the mother and father for survival. The vessel's, body's, mobility and strength is so minimal, the Soul requires others for survival. The five senses become soon the primary focus for the navigation and decision-making system of the Soul: the conscious awareness or mind.

The amount of input is overwhelming, the mind requires a lot of time to process the diverse experiences such as the taste of food coupled with if these tastes correspond with progress or decline. Which sounds require preparation for danger, which signal joy. Over time, the Souls begin to identify with their bodies, forgetting they are Souls in a simulation.

But why do Souls need vessels in the first place? And why is the "Life on Earth" simulation so uniquely suited for this purpose? The answer lies in the specific design of this simulation, which creates a structured and immersive environment for Souls to grow and evolve.

The "Life on Earth" simulation is just one of many simulations available to Souls. These simulations vary in structure, rules, and purpose, offering Souls a diverse range of experiences. Some simulations are highly structured, like "Life on Earth," with fixed rules for space, time, and physical laws. Others, like the dream-simulation, are more fluid, allowing for exploration beyond the constraints of physical reality. There are also simulations like remote viewing, which enable Souls to access information beyond their immediate environment, exploring shared memories, historical events, or even potential future timelines.

These simulations are not isolated realities but interconnected aspects of the Larger Consciousness System (LCS). They form a continuum of experience, with fluid boundaries that allow Souls to move between them seamlessly. Each simulation serves a unique purpose, helping

Souls grow and evolve through challenges, relationships, and the consequences of their choices.

In the next chapter, we'll explore the "Life on Earth", Dream, Remote Viewing and Near-Death Experience simulations in detail—its rules, its purpose, and how this provides a structured and immersive environment for Souls to experiences. We'll also examine how this simulation connects to other simulations, creating a rich and varied continuum of experience for Souls to explore.

1.2
Simulations Compared

The "Life on Earth" simulation is a structured and immersive simulation. It is meticulously designed with a specific set of rules governing space, time, memory, and interaction. Souls enter this simulation to experience growth through challenges, relationships, and the consequences of their choices.

Inside the "Life on Earth" simulation, two parts of you are simultaneously active: your mind and your Soul. At moments, you are thinking, logic, mentally focussed. One would call, in psychology, 'left brain' thinking. When you are more using your intuition or immersed in artistic endeavours, your "right brain" is more active. These left-right brain division I do not consider literal, but it is a useful metaphor.

In the examples below, there is a back-and-forth between being inside a simulation and being outside of a simulation. When I speak about being inside a simulation, I use the labels "you", "mind" and "conscious awareness". When I speak about being outside the simulation, I use the label "Soul". However, in, for example, the Near-Death Experience examples there is a gradual transgression from "you" to "Soul" and back to "you". In a Remote Viewing situation, there is a constant back-and-forth between the "you" and the "Soul".

It is always important to ask yourself when reading my or others' texts regarding a form of Simulation Theory: where am I? Am I now the Soul, or am I conscious awareness in the narrative?

The Life on Earth Simulation: tough and short

Ruleset of the "Life on Earth" Simulation
The simulation operates within a fixed framework of space and time. Space is three-dimensional, bound by physical laws like gravity, while time flows linearly from past to future. This creates a sense of continuity and causality, where actions have predictable consequences.

Souls connect to physical bodies (still virtual of course) with finite lifespans, this creates a sense of urgency and encourages meaningful choices within their allotted time.

The simulation is governed by strict physical laws—thermodynamics, electromagnetism, and biology—creating a stable and predictable environment, but also imposing constraints on what Souls can achieve.

Memory in the "Life on Earth" simulation is constrained. Souls have limited access to their broader Consciousness. Memories are not stored in the brain but pass through it as part of the simulation. The brain acts as a filter or interface, allowing the Soul to access memories stored at a higher, supra-level—such as the level of the Soul or the Larger Consciousness System.

Past-life memories are typically inaccessible, though some Souls may retain fragments or intuitive knowledge of their previous experiences.

The Soul's Experience in the Life on Earth Simulation
The Soul immerses fully in the simulation, closely identifying with its physical body and environmental rules. Yet, it remains unbound by them, operating as a transcendent entity that observes and influences the simulation from a higher plane of Consciousness.

For example, the Soul can send intuitive nudges or insights to the conscious mind (conscious awareness), bypassing the limitations of the brain. This is why people sometimes have "aha" moments or sudden realisations that seem to come from nowhere.

Similarly, the Soul can access visual data streams directly, allowing individuals to "see" without using their physical eyes. This demonstrates the Soul's ability to interact with the simulation in ways that defy its rules.

Why the Life on Earth Simulation Exists
The "Life on Earth" simulation serves as a training ground for Souls. It provides a structured environment where Souls can experience growth through challenges, relationships, and the consequences of their choices. The limitations of space, time, and memory create a sense of urgency and focus, encouraging Souls to make meaningful decisions within their lifespans.

The Dream-Simulation: A Playground for the Soul

Every night, when your body sleeps, your Soul switches attention towards the dream-simulation. This dream world is a virtual environment with rules that are very different from the "Life on Earth" simulation. While dreams often borrow elements from your waking life—familiar objects, people, and places—they twist and bend these elements in ways that defy the physical laws of Earth.

Some Characteristics of the Dream-Simulation
In the dream-simulation, space and time are fluid. One moment, you're in your childhood home, and the next, you're in a completely unfamiliar city. You can jump from one place to another instantly, or even shift perspectives—seeing yourself from a third-person view or stepping into someone else's shoes.

Gravity is optional; with a bit of practice, you can fly, float, or walk through walls. Objects might morph or change shape, and the environment can shift unpredictably.

Dreams follow a kind of emotional logic rather than physical logic. If you're afraid, the dream might generate a monster. If you're curious, it might create a door to explore.

Memory in the Dream-Simulation
Dream memories are fleeting and often fade quickly upon waking. However, with practice, you can train yourself to retain more of these memories.

Dreams frequently use symbols and metaphors to convey meaning. These symbols are drawn from your personal experiences and subconscious mind, which are accessed through the Soul's broader memory bank.

Why the Dream-Simulation Exists

The dream-simulation serves as a space where you can process emotions, explore ideas, and experiment with possibilities without the constraints of physical reality. It's also a place where the Soul can reconnect with its broader Consciousness, free from the limitations of the body. In a later chapter, I describe how dreams can function as a feedback mechanism and a way to measure an increase or decrease in entropy.

The Remote Viewing Simulation: Exploring Beyond the Physical

Another virtual environment that Souls can access is the remote viewing simulation. This is a more structured and less fluid reality than the dream-simulation, but it still operates under a different ruleset than "Life on Earth."

Remote viewing allows Souls to access information beyond their immediate physical environment, often related to shared memories, historical events, or even potential future timelines.

How Remote Viewing Works

Souls can tap into a kind of collective memory. They might "see" events from the past, present, or future, depending on their focus. Senses such as hearing, smelling, tasting and feeling can also be experienced during remote viewing.

The rules of remote viewing are influenced by the idea that future reality is probabilistic rather than fixed. A remote viewer picks up on the most likely or most significant events within a range of possibilities.

A viewer might shift between timelines as they focus on different probabilities. Unlike dreams, which are highly subjective, remote viewing aims for an emphasis on objectivity, and limits subjectivity. The viewer tries to separate their personal biases from the information they're receiving, but some level of interpretation is always involved.

Memory in the Remote Viewing Simulation

Remote viewers access a shared pool of information that transcends individual experiences. Past events are fixed whereas future events are probabilities, some much more likely to occur than others.

This memory is not tied to a specific brain or body but exists at a higher level of Consciousness. The information accessed in remote viewing is often probabilistic, reflecting potential outcomes rather than fixed events.

The conscious mind interprets the data stream it interacts with, inserting prejudice, assumptions and cultural bias to name a few. Personal memory is typically mingled with shared memory. The more a viewer practises, the better the chance of limiting this personal bias and prejudice.

Why Remote Viewing Exists

The remote viewing simulation serves as a tool for exploration and understanding. It allows the conscious mind, via the Soul, to gather information beyond their immediate physical reality.

Although remote viewing can be used in a daily operational setting, like work, the experience of accessing data beyond this simulation triggers for many people a fundamental shift in understanding reality. Like it did for me in a way.

Remote Viewing can also be used to make sense of the broader patterns and possibilities within the Larger Consciousness System.

In a later chapter, I explore remote viewing in great detail and offer concrete steps to try it yourself.

The Near-Death Experience Simulation: A Gateway to the Larger Consciousness System

Near-death experiences (NDEs) are profound and often life-altering events where the Soul begins to detach from the "Life on Earth" simulation and enters a transitional, dream-like environment. This simulation operates under a unique ruleset, like in dreams, blending elements of the physical and non-physical realms

It serves as a bridge, a room if you will, between the structured reality of Earth and the fluid, expansive nature of the Larger Consciousness System (LCS).

Characteristics of the Near-Death Experience Simulation

In an NDE, the Soul begins to disengage (switch data stream) from the physical body, often triggered by trauma, illness, or other extreme conditions. As this happens, the rules of the "Life on Earth" simulation—such as gravity, time, and physical limitations—start to dissolve.

The Soul switches focus to a space where time becomes elastic, stretching or compressing in ways that defy linear understanding. Space, too, becomes fluid; individuals regularly report moving through tunnels, floating above their bodies, or transitioning to otherworldly landscapes.

The environment in an NDE is, at first, often shaped by the Soul's emotional and spiritual state. The conscious aware mind might still carry emotions from for example a traumatic event, like an accident, into this other simulation.

Interestingly enough, an NDE experience does follow for a long period a "Life on Earth" chronological experience. That is, during NDE events, the experiencer's timeline runs synchronous with the timeline of "Life on Earth". The time experience might very well be compressed or expanded during the experience, but the start and end are the same.

Memory in the Near-Death Experience Simulation

Memories during an NDE are vivid and often more accessible than in the "Life on Earth" simulation. The Soul's connection to its broader Consciousness is heightened, allowing it to access a deeper level of understanding.

Many who return from an NDE report a sense of clarity and insight that persists long after the event. They regularly describe feeling more connected to their true essence and purpose, as if the experience has lifted a veil between the physical and non-physical realms.

However, like dreams, NDE memories can fade upon returning to the physical body. The brain, acting as a filter, struggles to fully process and retain the vastness of the experience. Yet, even fragmented memories can have a transformative impact, regularly leading to profound shifts in perspective, values, and behaviour.

Why the Near-Death Experience Simulation Exists

The NDE simulation serves as a transitional space, offering the Soul a glimpse of the Larger Consciousness System while still tethered to the physical body. It provides an opportunity *for reflection, healing, and growth, often prompting individuals to reevaluate their lives and priorities.*

For some, it's a reminder of their true nature and purpose, helping them reconnect with their Soul's broader journey. NDEs also act as a kind of "reset button," allowing the Soul to release old patterns or traumas that no longer serve its growth. This can lead to significant changes in personality, relationships, and worldview.

For those who return to the "Life on Earth" simulation, the experience often brings a renewed sense of meaning and direction, as well as a more profound understanding of the interconnectedness of all things

The Role of the Soul in the Near-Death Experience Simulation
During an NDE, the distinction between conscious awareness and the Soul blurs. You are aware of what happens during your NDE and memories, from a few to everything, are retrievable after the NDE.

During the NDE, you connect to yet another part of Consciousness, free from the constraints of the physical body. You can access data streams that are normally filtered out by the mind, such as intuitive insights, past-life memories, or glimpses of future possibilities.

Your ability to move between simulations is particularly evident in NDEs. As the physical body (still virtual) approaches death, you begin to shift its focus from the "Life on Earth" simulation to the more fluid environment of the NDE. This transition is often seamless, with you adapting to the new ruleset without conscious effort.

The Near-Death Experience Simulation in the Continuum
NDEs are not isolated events but part of the fluid continuum of simulations within the Larger Consciousness System. They represent a transitional state, where the Soul begins to detach from the structured reality of Earth and explore the more expansive realms of Consciousness. This makes them a unique and valuable tool for understanding the interconnected nature of all simulations.

By experiencing an NDE, the mind, you, gains a more in-depth understanding of its true nature and purpose, as well as the broader patterns and possibilities within the LCS. This knowledge can then be integrated into the "Life on Earth" simulation, enriching the Soul's journey and helping it navigate the challenges and opportunities of physical existence. In this way, NDEs serve as a bridge between the physical and non-physical.

The Interconnected Simulations: A Fluid Continuum of Experience

While we've discussed the "Life on Earth," "Dream," and "Remote Viewing" and "Near-Death Experience" simulations as distinct environments, it's important to understand that these are not separate, isolated realities. Instead, they are interconnected aspects of the Larger Consciousness System (LCS), each with its ruleset and data stream, but all part of the same overarching environment. The boundaries between them are fluid, and the Soul can move between them seamlessly, often without realising it.

> *The Continuum of Simulations*
> *Imagine the Larger Consciousness System as a vast, interconnected network of simulations, each with its 'flavour' or ruleset. These simulations are not rigidly divided but rather blend into one another, creating a continuum of experience.*
>
> *For example, "Life on Earth" is among the examples of the most structured and immersive simulation, with fixed rules for space, time, and physical laws. Dreams are less structured, with fluid rules for space, time, and physics, but they still borrow elements from the "Life on Earth" simulation.*
>
> *Remote viewing is more structured than dreams but less rigid than "Life on Earth," allowing for exploration beyond the immediate physical environment. Intuition, clairvoyance, and extra-ocular vision are subtle shifts within the "Life on Earth" simulation, where the Soul accesses data streams that bypass the usual sensory filters.*
>
> *Near-death experiences (NDEs) are transitional states where the Soul begins to detach from the "Life on Earth" simulation and enters a more fluid, dream-like environment.*
>
> *How the Simulations Blend*
> *The rulesets of these simulations are not mutually exclusive. For example, during a dream, you might experience elements of remote viewing or clairvoyance, accessing information beyond your immediate environment. Similarly, in waking*

life, you might have moments of intuition, where the rules of the "Life on Earth" simulation are temporarily overridden.

The transitions between simulations are often seamless. When you fall asleep, you don't suddenly "leave" the "Life on Earth" simulation and "enter" the dream-simulation. Instead, your awareness gradually shifts from one ruleset to another, blending the two experiences.

When you are in an accident, you not necessarily "leave the body" at once or "leave the Earth" at once. You now perceive your physical body to be on this physical Earth, during an NDE though you become the observer of your body and Earth. The longer you are in the NDE state, the less you identify with the physical simulation, and the more you begin to return to your original state; Soul.

Memories are not confined to a single simulation but exist at a higher, supra-level. This means that experiences from one simulation can influence or inform experiences in another. For example, a dream might help you process emotions or gain insights that you later apply in waking life.

The Role of the Soul in Navigating the Continuum
The Soul is not bound by the rules of any single simulation. Instead, it exists as a superset, able to access and interact with multiple simulations simultaneously. This is why phenomena like intuition, clairvoyance, and extra-ocular vision are possible—the Soul is tapping into data streams that exist beyond the constraints of the "Life on Earth" simulation.

In the case of extra-ocular experience (seeing without eyes)s, your conscious awareness (mind) does not receive information through the eyes as you are blind or blindfolded. But there is a will and intent to "see", and the mind can be trained to switch to another data-stream.

Take reading letters on a page. These are, within this simulation, nothing more or less than virtual letters, on a virtual page. When you move your awareness outside this reality—switching data-stream—you can access any data. Thus, you can also access the virtual letters on the virtual page, and this is how you "see".

Some shifts between simulations happen automatically, such as when you fall asleep and enter the dream-simulation or enter an NDE state. In these cases, the Soul adjusts its focus without conscious effort. Other shifts require conscious *effort, such as practicing remote viewing, extra-ocular vision or developing intuition. In these cases, the Soul must learn to quiet the 5-senses and tune into the desired data stream.*

The continuum of simulations exists to provide the Soul with a rich and varied range of experiences. Each simulation offers a different perspective and set of challenges, helping the Soul grow and evolve. By moving between these simulations, the Soul gains a more profound understanding of itself and the Larger Consciousness System.

One of the hardest ideas to grasp is how you can be fully immersed in a simulation—like "Life on Earth"—while your Soul exists as something larger, a superset of that simulation. The Soul isn't confined to the rules or limitations of any single reality. Instead, it operates at a higher level, accessing and interacting with multiple simulations at once.

Think of the Soul as the "player" in the earlier described video game. The character in the game (your physical body) is bound by the game's rules—gravity, time, and physical limitations. But the player (your Soul) exists outside the game and can influence it in ways that seem impossible within the game's framework.

This work seeks to unify the non-physical and physical, framing the Self (the union of Soul and "you") as your higher identity—so enmeshed in the "Earth simulation" it forgets its essence—with a dedicated chapter ("The Soul") expanding this concept through an alternate lens.

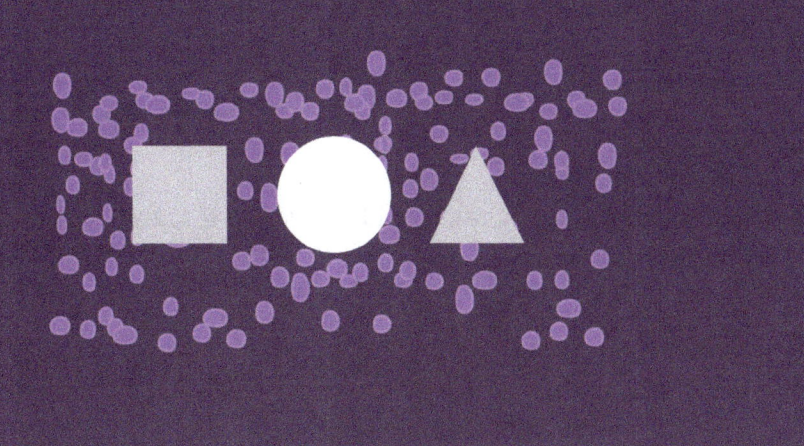

1.3
Consciousness is Fundamental

While "Consciousness is fundamental" sets the foundational premise that everything originates from Consciousness, the LCS (Local Consciousness System) is the implementation of this concept. It provides the structure through which fundamental Consciousness manifests and organises itself into an interactive, evolving system. Everything that exists emerges from this fundamental Consciousness. Consciousness evolves too, and so does the LCS. This concept of an emerging awareness is not new. Jacob Böhme, a 16th-century German shoemaker, thinker, and mystic, from what is now Poland, had profound insights into the origin of reality centuries ago.

In his book Aurora, Böhme explores the nature of God and creation, presenting God as a dynamic, self-revealing process rather than a static being. For Böhme, God's unfolding involves a continual desire for self-awareness and manifestation. He imagined this unfolding happening through the interplay of opposites—such as Darkness and Light, Good and Evil—forces that, in their tension, give rise to the dynamics of creation. These opposites are not considered mere contradictions but as complementary forces necessary for the realisation and revelation of the divine. Through their interaction,

God's nature becomes manifest and is continually revealed in creation.

Böhme's vision of God as an unfolding process through the interaction of opposites suggests that reality is not a static, predetermined system, but one that is dynamic and evolving. Similarly, Tom's concept of the Larger Consciousness System (LCS) proposes a reality that evolves through the flow of data and information, where Consciousness is the fundamental driving force. In both models, the unfolding of awareness is central—whether it's the divine unfolding through creation in Böhme's cosmology or the evolving informational structure of the LCS in Campbell's framework. Everything in the LCS consists of data or information, evolving as the system itself learns and adapts. A big problem with the "data and information" metaphor is that people would relate this to computers and software and forget it is a metaphor.

Furthermore, there are theories and philosophies that suggest we are, in fact, inside a real computer, something I strongly disagree with. Placing Consciousness inside a computer is another way to circle us back into the Physicalism, and the same fundamental questions are not answered. Others use a metaphor such as "energy" or "light" or "hologram" or "vibrations". Those labels would then suggest that Consciousness is an aspect of a physical reality.

> *Allow me to explain this, I need to make an important distinction between using 'data and information' metaphor in the 'Life on Earth' context, or in the LCS context. The words I have to use, such as data and information and so on, are "Life on Earth" concepts. There is no way of knowing if the LCS has also data and information as we understand them. When I speak of, for example, the above words in context with the LCS, have an open mind.*

In the logic of the LCS, data refers to raw, unprocessed symbols and facts. Like building blocks or the raw ingredients that the LCS uses to create meaning. For instance, numbers, letters, words, or even raw sensory input like an image or sound wave make up data. Information is what you get when data is processed, organised, or structured to provide meaning. Meaning emerges when Consciousness interprets data and assigns significance to it. For example, putting the raw data of hitting your toe into context to create pain information. Consciousness interprets that data into information. Without a conscious entity to make sense of the raw data, it remains just a collection of symbols. The LCS is non-physical, and therefore it won't feel if you hit your toe. Via your Soul, the LCS registers your reaction, your emotions, and intentions. Do you get upset, blame others, or react in another manner?

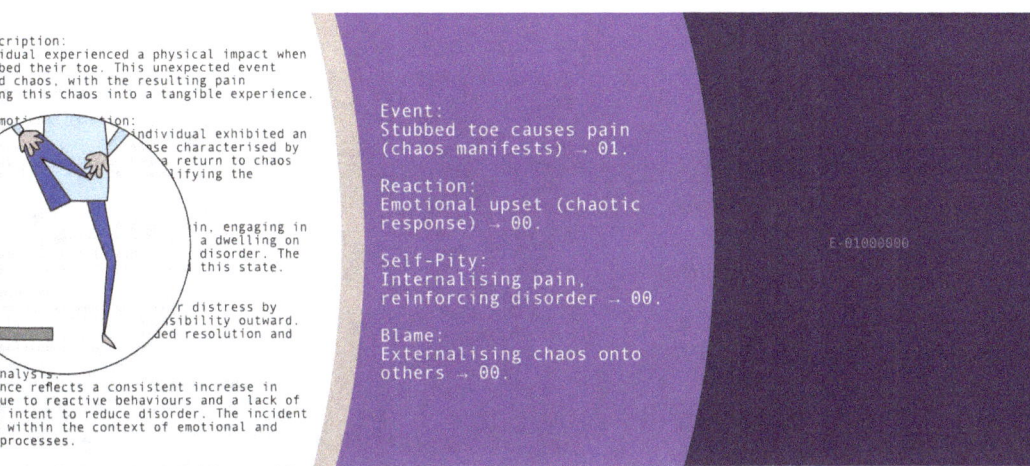

The pain you feel by hitting your toe is a data stream or sequence of data. This pain feels real, as within this simulation, it is real. Things that happen inside this simulation are as real as they can get. All the interactions you have with the environment, the speed you move your foot, the hardness of the object you hit, and much more is inside this stream of data. I go more into the toe example in a following chapter. Now take the ink marks on this page (or dark or light pixels on your screen)— the letters and symbols themselves. An isolated letter caries little meaning; a few randomly ordered letters mean very little if anything. But when these letters are ordered in a way you recognise as a word, meaning emerges. In the context of the LCS and information theory in general, high(er) entropy is converted into low(er) entropy. Order is created out of chaos, Ordo et Chao.

The LCS seeks to reduce entropy and create more order. High entropy represents disorder and randomness, while low entropy is associated with order and structure. A central theme in Tom's model is that Consciousness evolves by lowering its entropy. Another way of saying the same is that the LCS tries to define itself. Ill-defined data is chaotic, random, perhaps. This random or chaotic data cannot do anything and does not add to creating meaning. The goal of the LCS is to evolve into something meaningful, ergo: stimulate order. It means moving from disorder (self-centredness, fear) toward order (cooperation, love). Higher quality states of Consciousness correlate with lower entropy. When you act out of love, you're working to lower the chaos within Consciousness.

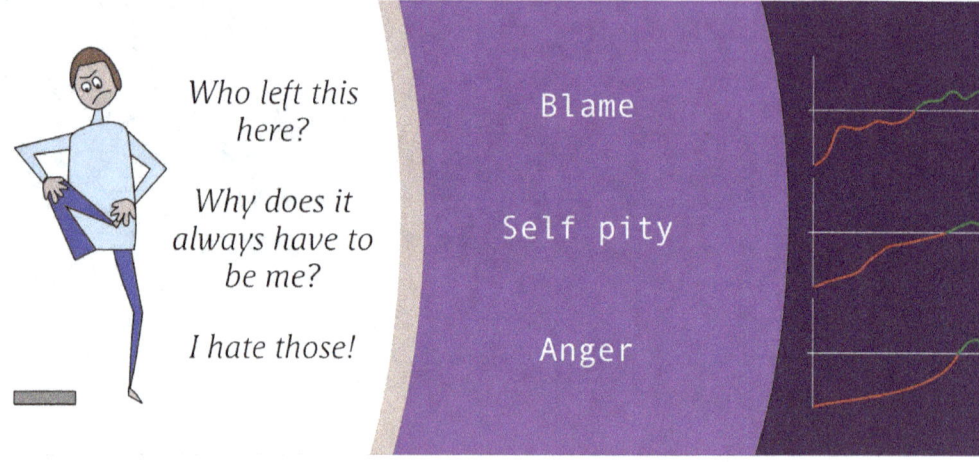

Each of us is an Individuated Unit of Consciousness (IUoC), a self-aware entity capable of making choices that affect the direction of our growth. All these IUoC (Souls) are collectively part of the LCS, providing the environment and structure that facilitate the growth and exchange of information among all Consciousness units. The word I use is Soul, but it means the same as Tom's IUoC. Our decisions contribute to the evolution of both ourselves and the LCS. The Soul always remains inside Consciousness, and when a Soul wants to experience the virtual reality game "Life on Earth", then an instance of the Soul is dedicated to fully engage in this experience. Although the instance – you– and your Soul are still part of the same entity, you experience yourself primarily through your five senses, and within this physical reality.

Your awareness of the LCS is very minimal unless there is, for example, a reason to let you pay extra attention to the existence of the

LCS. Moments of intense trauma or crisis could trigger, for example, a near-death experience in which the data from the LCS stays with you after you return to conscious awareness again. But every night you open up to another kind of data stream from the LCS when you dream. If you meditate or do remote viewing, you become aware of other types of data. An important deciding factor in these differences is your intention, like in remote viewing you actively go after data, or as in dreams it could be more like passive feedback on your state of growth.

Data does not travel from A to B within the LCS; data comes into existence and becomes available. The LCS does not start beyond what we describe as "the universe"; the universe is within the LCS. The universe is a subset of the LCS and evolves as well, depending on how conscious beings interact with this universe. Experiments in quantum physics suggest that even within our simulation, there are circumstances where space and time behave very differently than we re-used to in everyday life. One such observation goes by the name of "entanglement". The theory of entanglement describes how when a small particle is split into two other particles, and whatever happens to one particle instantly affects the other particle. Distance seems not to matter either.

Thus, somehow and under specific circumstances, we can initiate, influence and observe how time and space collapse. Another quantum effect is what is called the Observer effect. This suggests that your conscious awareness influences physical reality, on the level of particles and waves. When I combine these two observations and conclusions, I could imagine that conscious awareness and intent influence physical reality, instantly and anywhere.

In other words, your intentions, emotions, and thoughts influence the world around you, right now and not limited by distance. This makes you wonder, doesn't it?

Free will
Every Soul has free will and is self-aware; this allows you to make choices that shape your experiences and contribute to your growth. This growth is both for you in this lifetime and for your Soul as a whole over multiple lifetimes. The intentions behind the doing, the action, have a bigger impact on the growth of the Soul than the doing or action itself. In this simulation, however, the doing and the action is what others react to. This is how it seems, at first at least, and we get to this later.

You are an instance of the Soul; you experience "Life on Earth" together with many other instances whose Souls are elsewhere in the LCS too. On Earth, you interact with others and with the surrounding environment, including nature and animals. Your five senses are the dominating receptors for information you receive from the environment and others. Your interactions and actions matter mostly in your current life, where you affect other instances—people and animals. Later in this book, I dive into this fascinating concept of the Soul and life.

This book emphasises the role of free will and the importance of understanding the limiting factors inside this simulation. My theory is that when you begin to see what pulls and pushes at you, you can also begin to decide which of those pulls and pushes are beneficial or detrimental to your growth. An important question is, if you are pulled and pushed without you realising this, into directions you are made to believe you want, do you then still exercise free will?

Intentions

From the LCS' perspective, your intentions matter more than actions. Intentions are about the reason you do things. Every so often the intentions are good, but the action that follows turns out to be detrimental to someone else, or yourself. The opposite could also happen, of course. Then there is a fascinating concept of "mind over matter", which suggests that your thinking or intentions actually influences "stuff" around you. Now we enter the territory of real magic(k). Intentions, thoughts, and words follow a logical sequence, and emotions fit somewhere in between that sequence. Let me give an example, a crude example, but it demonstrates how words affect matter in a real and verifiable sense.

A kind word you speak to your loved one triggers a physiological response; perhaps Oxytocin (Dopamine, Serotonin, Endorphins) is released and a feeling of warmth, happiness, and safety emerges in the body of your loved one. This is a sequence from hearing, to comprehending, the release of various chemical components and bioelectrical pulses which results in the conscious awareness of what you could describe as an emotion.

Your intention alone plays a role too, as especially when we are close to someone, the other sense those intentions. Picking up these intentions could even precede the words that you speak to the other. A mismatch between intention and spoken words could result in confusion, or uncertainty.

> *Presentiment studies show that humans sense from roughly 10 seconds to 3 seconds before seeing an image if the image shows something upsetting or neutral. The body responds while the mind is clueless and can only guess.*
>
> Julia Mossbridge et al.
> 2011
> Predictive physiological anticipation preceding
> seemingly unpredictable stimuli: a meta-analysis

The idea that the mind modifies matter further reinforces this connection between your intentions and the body, your own or that of others. As suggested with the observer effect. When love is expressed as compassion and care, it can profoundly influence your reality. Whether it's through the placebo effect or the positive impact of nurturing relationships on well-being, the underlying physics proposes that our intentions—which are deeply tied to love—shape our experiences.

The Observer Effect
The observer effect refers to the idea that the act of observation influences the outcome of what is being observed. Within Tom Campbell's Larger Consciousness System (LCS), this concept extends beyond the physical realm to encompass Consciousness and intent.

At its essence, the observer effect reveals that reality is neither entirely objective nor independent of us. For example, in quantum mechanics, a particle's state remains undefined until it is measured, suggesting that observation actively shapes outcomes. Similarly, in the LCS framework, our intent and awareness influence the probabilities of events, highlighting the participatory nature of reality.

Practically, this means that the focus of your attention and the quality of your intent shape both your personal experiences and the broader reality. Observing with fear, doubt, or negativity reinforces those patterns, while observing with clarity, love, and purpose aligns you with lower-entropy, more harmonious outcomes.

Recognising the observer effect empowers you to take responsibility for your role in shaping reality. It encourages you to be aware of your intentions, emotions and thoughts, reminding you that your awareness is not passive but an active force—albeit often very small—in creating your life and the world around you.

Authenticity and Fear
When intention and action align, there is more impact on this reality and on the Soul level. When you are consciously aware of your intentions and consciously choose what actions to take, you get close to living authentically. If you also follow your Soul's desires, authenticity is within reach. There is a large spectrum of variations, such as you have intentions that are not truly yours. Strong beliefs or habits can cloud your awareness of what you truly want.

When you remove fears, your intentions are more authentic, and more authentic intentions and actions accelerate change. Positive change means you care for yourself and for others; you are empathetic and cooperative–lowering the entropy and this means you grow. Negative change implies self-interest; it is about you; you are self-focused and often divisive– you raise entropy and degrade. Tom uses the words love for positive growth and fear of negative decline. In this virtual reality framework, love isn't some abstract, fluffy emotion—it's an organised, low-entropy state of being. Interactions based on love create order and cultivate cooperation, allowing Consciousness to evolve. Your love-based and fear-based intentions and actions affect the overall change of the LCS.

In the realm of physics, fear leads to high-entropy states—think conflict, stress, and chaos. Love, as a low-entropy outcome, promotes trust, connection, and growth. The laws of the universe, like the second law of thermodynamics, echo this concept. Without conscious input, systems naturally trend toward increased disorder unless they align with the principles of connecting through love.

Probability

Probability defines the range of possible outcomes available to conscious entities. This concept lies at the heart of the LCS's non-deterministic nature, where reality unfolds not as a predetermined sequence but as a flexible set of possibilities, each influenced by the unique intentions and decisions of conscious beings. Experiences emerge based on these probable outcomes, aligning with the LCS's evolutionary aim to reduce entropy. This framework encourages growth, development, and a higher level of order within Consciousness. In the LCS, some outcomes are just much more likely than other outcomes.

In our simulated environment, "Life on Earth", gravity is a good example. According to the rule-set for this simulation, stuff is pulled (or pushed) towards the centre of the planet. And once this rule was once observed by a conscious entity inside this simulation, this rule could not be undone any more. That is another important aspect of the LCS: once observed, it cannot be unobserved. This is needed to guarantee coherence and consistency. Other simulations might have an opposite "gravity". Perhaps you are pulled or pushed outwards, and the ground you rest on is on the outside. Like being inside a football and being forced against the inner lining of the ball.

You influence reality with your intentions, emotions, words and actions, but this is not some wishing well where the LCS gives whatever your heart desires. In a later chapter, I talk about the mechanism behind manifesting. This explains the difference between wishing and the underlying mechanics of manifestation. Regardless, you do influence the world around you. How likely your influence creates the outcome you look for depends on various mechanisms. We get to those.

Experiencing Reality Through the LCS

Life on Earth is a challenging simulation. Our experiences feel tangible; they follow structured rules that people describe as laws, like the law of gravity. The scientific method is an appropriate framework for validating established principles (laws) and identifying irregularities or deviations (anomalies). Reality operates under consistent principles, such as gravity, touch, and sound. These are part of the rules for this simulation we are in. Other simulations might have wholly unique rules. Imagine tasting sounds, hearing colour and smelling touches. Hard to imagine, I know.

We perceive time as linear, as cause and effect. You do something, something else happens. The LCS allows for multiple experiences that do not necessarily fit a conventional understanding of time. Some experiences, such as dreams, intuition, or remote viewing, propose that other aspects of Consciousness are not bound by physical laws. In your dream, you receive data from the LCS without too much interference in the mind. Your mind is largely inactive (asleep); it remains primarily alert to potential threats. During this state, certain senses, like smell, continue to function effectively. Remote viewing is a technique and protocol where you actively listen to data streams coming in through your unconscious mind and interpret them with your conscious mind.

There exist numerous modalities, techniques, and states of being that facilitate both passive and active engagement with the LCS. You encourage the interaction, the enquiring and even influencing of the LCS, either passively, actively or through a form in between. To engage meaningfully, practices can help in connecting to others in the LCS, Souls of other realities or to people within the simulation you are in now. For the LCS, meaningful interactions are about nurturing love, and this is best achieved when you know what you really want, limiting external influence. The LCS is not concerned with how you achieve that state of authentically loving being.

Inside this simulation, many tools are available, many lessons and paths you can follow. The primary goal for you is to align your conscious thoughts and actions with your true self or Soul. This requires the courage to confront personal fears and societal expectations, choosing actions that genuinely reflect who you are. I define this as "becoming authentic", which is a state that is not achievable by participating in one game "Life on Earth". You should strive to become authentic though in this life, and in a following life, new challenges are on the agenda. In this chain of birth and rebirth, you have the opportunities to grow a multitude of facets, overcome many kinds of fears and to grow in love for others. You need many lives to overcome these fears, and when you have accomplished that, you are truly authentic on a Soul level. Then you move on to another kind of simulation. But before you have reached that stage, the LCS, the rule-set within this simulation and others with their free will, shall challenge, provoke and tempt you.

There is a lot more to the LCS and that is why Tom wrote three books and produced many videos, did many workshops and gave numerous interviews. I restrict myself to the bare bones So that this book keeps its focus.

2
The Soul

Bridging the Abstract and the Real: Understanding Soul Dynamics

In the previous chapter, I described how to understand the LCS and what your role is, and hinted at the role of your Soul. This chapter looks closer at the Soul and how it functions and evolves within the LCS. The Soul is abstract; you do not have a jar on the shelf with your Soul inside. Much of this book is abstract and, for some, perhaps vague, as the topics cannot be described in physical, five sense terminology. The LCS, the Soul, love, and intentions remain elusive, and the best we can do is to observe the effects of actions and use logic to build a working model of this reality.

You know what love feels like: the love for a spouse, a child, an animal. You can give your love even a grade. Your love for your pet scores likely higher than the love for the potato on your plate, or the other way around if you were starving. This love you cannot bring into a scientific laboratory and measure objectively; the love you feel is subjective. But it is real and of a different order. The intensity of love you feel for your pet shall be different for other people who do not have that bond with your pet. A scientist cannot take "your love" and replicate that with other people. Other people will have their love for their pet (or potato).

The actions or reactions you show regarding your loved one and others you can observe, and it is from this kind of observation that we use to deduce what love comes from and how it manifests. The same for fears and a whole plethora of feelings, emotions, and thoughts. Our physical body is a wonderful entity to study and map biological processes with, for example, emotions. This is in many situations a bidirectional interaction; biological states or changes result in an emotion, and emotions result in biological states or changes. Humanity has come a long way to understand this interaction.

From the perspective of the LCS, this biological–emotional mapping is one of the subsets of reality in this simulation. This interaction is real, within this simulation, but it is not the ultimate reality. Thus, a sad thought can cause you to start to cry. Hitting your toes can cause you to feel pain and perhaps swear. These are real experiences, but the LCS suggests that these are simulated experiences–still feeling real to you– to help you grow through choices. You can observe this growth (or decline) in this life; the Soul is the accumulation of the qualities of these experiences across lifetimes.

The Soul collects, structures, and stores these qualities, contributing to the LCS—a limitless dynamic database of experiences and knowledge contributed to by all souls. The LCS enables the free flow of information, allowing each Soul access not only to its experiences but also to insights from the collective pool of Consciousness. A Soul cannot directly access the data stored in another Soul; your data is private. But, if there is an agreement on the Soul level to exchange data, you could tap into another person's data stream or stored data.

If you have a connection on a deep emotional level with a loved one, you can pick up data from that person. This data comes in the form of insights, feelings and intuitions, for example. At such moments, there is an agreement to "open up" to one another. This interconnectedness stimulates mutual growth, as each individual's experiences become part of a larger ecosystem. This enriches not only the souls directly involved, but also the entire system. Through this form of private/open access, the LCS supports individual and collective evolution from one lifetime to the next.

This concept of agreement needs some explanation. It is common to think of an agreement as something two or more people verbalised, or signed. But from a Soul's perspective an agreement is also when you participate, accept, or not consciously deny a certain interaction. For example, when you "go along" with a ritual even though you do not really like it, but group pressure is too much for you to withstand: you are in agreement. Conformity, intellectual laziness, pleasing are also forms of agreement, no need to sign a paper.

The Soul System

Your life has a beginning and an end, and a beginning again, and so forth. The Soul is a constant; it remains, while many instances go through experiences in "Life on Earth" or elsewhere. It makes sense to see the Soul as something non-physical from this human (you) perspective. The analogy of the LCS, and thus the Soul, to be an information system is logical, as information can be collected, structured, stored, and later disseminated in various forms through various channels. Information can be compressed to enhance efficiency. Information can be turned into logic and algorithms. Your repetitive reactions are captured as a formula, an algorithm and stored.

Imagine you are unfortunate to hit your toe twice a week for a whole year. The system would either have to store individual experiences twice for each of the 52 weeks, which makes 104 experiences to be stored. Instead, the LCS creates the experience-package "hit toe plus the same reactions" and adds x 104 for the times it happens. At the Soul level, a conclusion (Soul quality) could be: the incarnated me is a slow learner when it comes to hitting toes and reactions. Take this example with a grain of salt, but I hope you get the overall idea.

A Soul as part of an information system makes sense. The benefits are efficiency, flexibility and actually pragmatism. The Soul is not drawn into a web of emotions and reactions, like you are. Emotions and pain, for example, are part of the subset–Life on Earth– and thus felt by you. The Soul registers and merges the essential data and information with itself. When you accept the idea that the Soul is part of an information system, it makes sense to think of the Soul as being described with data, but not data itself.

Now at this point you might wonder, "am I some software running in some far away computer?" No, you are not, far from it as the real you, your Soul, is a highly advanced evolving entity with infinite potential. And the real–your Soul– you choose to accelerate learning in the simulation "Life on Earth", where you are now. In this simulation, you have, in fact, limited potential. You have a limited lifespan, limited senses, and limited understanding.

Soul Learning

You're here to learn, grow, and accomplish what you've set out to do. Your response to things that don't go the way you want tells the Soul and the LCS where you are in your development. However, fear and ego can obscure the insight that you have access to this more profound wisdom. As you read about this different world-view of Consciousness and the LCS, you can then learn about how to intentionally interact with this LCS. You do interact unintentionally already, thoughts that you get about others that turned out to be relevant, only you did not pay any attention. Or the common situation where you just think of someone and then the person calls, or sends you a message.

Learning is the domain of the physical world and the mind. This learning is often helped by intuition or insight, a direct tap into the knowledge base of the LCS. Your mind works as a filter for the incoming and the outgoing data, from and to the LCS. Consider the mind as a radio that can tune into different channels. For some frequency bands, you need a standard antenna, one that comes with the radio. But for other frequency bands you require different antennas as to receive a clearer signal. You can develop this "different antenna" and receive a clearer signal.

As your entropy goes down, and thus becomes more loving and caring, your "different antenna", your intuition and connection to the LCS become stronger. There is no need to do any "hocus-pocus". As you become more loving and caring, and more authentic, your connection grows. You grow within a lifetime, and your Soul grows consequently too. You set goals to accomplish for a particular life before and during your life. Likewise, you measure the difference between the start and end, and that difference is your actual growth. Sometimes you grow into a positive direction, sometimes into a negative direction. That is okay, as many factors play a role in your development. You have many paths towards working towards your goal, such as dealing with frustration, and many external factors influence you. And on each of those paths, you encounter others with their free will, doing their thing.

Soul Qualities

Frustration is one of the many "qualities" you can work on; greed, excessive generosity, lust and excessive chastity are a few other such human qualities. Life on Earth presents endless challenges and variations throughout a lifetime. Imagine how many challenges you will face across many subsequent lives. If you are born into a wealthy family, generosity seems like an easy quality to have. However, even though you have the financial wealth you need, the culture and values that surround you might encourage greed. If you grow up poor, you may be encouraged to help others because it is good for both of you to help each other. Variations of environments, cultures, and challenges are many.

All of the many qualities you can work on, I lead back to two core fears: that of abandonment and the end of existence. These low-level fears give rise, at a higher level, to emotions, thoughts, and possibly actions. The fear of abandonment can be presented at a higher level, as forms of jealousy where you feverishly try to "protect" what you think you have, or have a right to. Your fears, emotions, thoughts, and actions cause reactions in others. And so you, and I, are in constant interaction with ourselves and others. All these interactions lead to choices, and the quality of these choices reflects the direction of your growth within one life, and above all, the cumulative growth of your Soul.

Like you should not force the behaviour of those around you, The LCS should not, and does not, force the behaviour of the souls in its environment. The idea that you should force someone to do what you want them to do is based on a few high-level emotions, which ultimately can be deduced to fear of abandonment or end of existence. Forced behaviour encourages fear, not positive growth. This cycle of fear-based reactions can be broken; however, it necessitates an understanding and acceptance of a form of reality such as proposed by Tom's LCS. The most important thing is to understand and accept that you are never alone and that you do not go away.

We play a long game in a complex network of space, time, and interactions. You might already understand the reason many lifetimes are needed.

2.1
Birth, Death, and Rebirth
The Cycles of Existence and the Path to Authenticity

For nihilists, there's no existence after death. Monotheistic religions offer an afterlife, but it's only accessible after death. Both views ultimately boil down to one life, one chance. The main difference is when rewards are offered: before or after death.

This chapter examines life, death, and rebirth, highlighting their importance in the Larger Consciousness System (LCS). It explores how these concepts nurture Soul evolution and growth. For some, this perspective aligns with Near-Death Experiences (NDE), while for others, it offers a rational and understandable view of reincarnation. NDEs challenge the idea of reincarnation as a superstitious or primitive concept, presenting it as a natural, logical process. The term "reincarnation" comes from Latin and means "being made flesh again" in modern English.

Rebirth is a concept that bridges ancient beliefs with modern metaphysical frameworks like Tom Campbell's Larger Consciousness System (LCS). In the LCS, rebirth represents the process through which individuated units of consciousness (IUOCs) participate in multiple lifetimes, reducing entropy and evolving through conscious choices toward love and authenticity.

Historical Alignments

Animism and Ancient Nordic traditions offer unique perspectives on life, death, and spiritual continuity. Animism, prevalent in many indigenous cultures, sees all elements of nature as imbued with spirit and consciousness. This worldview suggests a cyclical relationship between life, death, and rebirth, where the Soul may merge with nature or take on various forms.

Similarly, in Ancient Nordic traditions, the concept of reincarnation exists subtly. There are beliefs in the cycle of the Soul and the idea that the Soul could return to the world, either through familial lineage or as part of nature's ongoing flow. The Nordic notion of Valhalla and the eventual Ragnarok (the end of the world and its rebirth) presents a cyclical view of life and death, where death marks a transformation. This aligns with the LCS's perspective on spiritual evolution through recurring experiences.

Ancient traditions like Hinduism and Buddhism have centralised rebirth in their doctrine of Samsara, where the Soul cycles through lifetimes, driven by karma, toward liberation. Theosophy similarly views reincarnation as part of the Soul's evolutionary journey. Gnosticism and Catharism introduce a form of rebirth through spiritual awakening, where the Soul transcends ignorance and returns to the divine. These views align with the LCS's idea of growth through multiple lifetimes.

Christianity, Islam, and Judaism became less explicit about reincarnation, focusing instead on spiritual renewal and resurrection. Christianity's resurrection and Judaism's mystical teachings on gilgul neshamot (Soul transmigration) suggest a form of spiritual rebirth. Islam emphasises the Soul's growth through trials and purification, a process that loosely aligns with the idea of spiritual progression across multiple lifetimes, resonating with the LCS's view of learning through experience.

Rebirth, once largely dismissed in the modern scientific and philosophical world, has gradually found its place in contemporary thought, with many notable figures acknowledging its potential reality. This shift in perspective reflects a growing openness to ideas that transcend traditional materialism, leading to a broader acceptance of reincarnation as a concept worth exploring. Some 20th and 21st century's most influential thinkers, including scientists and philosophers, have come to recognise the possibility of reincarnation, not just as a spiritual belief, but also as a logical and coherent part of the human experience.

Carl Jung, the Swiss psychiatrist, explored reincarnation through his work on the collective unconscious, suggesting that the Soul could experience continuity across lifetimes, contributing to spiritual evolution. Similarly, Dr Ian Stevenson dedicated his career to researching reincarnation, documenting thousands of cases where children recalled past lives with remarkable accuracy and challenging materialist views of consciousness. Dr. Elisabeth Kübler-Ross, through her work on near-death experiences, also supported the idea of reincarnation, seeing it as part of the Soul's continuous journey. Dr. Carol Bowman expanded on Stevenson's research, documenting numerous cases of children with specific, verifiable memories of past lives, further legitimising reincarnation as a tangible phenomenon.

Past Lives

The belief in multiple lifetimes and reincarnation has its flaws, including amusing ones. For example, those who believe in it tend to discuss their past lives, leading some to inflate the significance of their past −accomplishments compared to their current ones. Someone may claim to have been a priestess in Atlantis, implying they are special. I was actually a humble cobbler sometime around 1600, in Görlitz, Poland, and wrote texts in my spare time. It's a joke, some people may understand.

There are many compelling accounts of children who remember their previous lives. They can describe their families, their names, where they lived, important life events, and even how they died. If the story involves a recent past life, it is not uncommon for the details to be corroborated. The psychiatrist Ian Stevenson has written numerous articles and books on this subject.

The idea that young children can recall their previous lives in the context of the LCS makes sense. In the early stages of a child's development, the connection with the LCS is still more accessible. Later in life, factors such as social conditioning and physiological changes in the body can make the LCS connection less accessible. However, you can maintain it and even improve it, but only if you take deliberate and conscious actions.

My first question about a story of a specific past life is: is this about **your** past life, or **a** past life? I propose this as a good first question, as from the LCS perspective, you benefit from lowering your entropy, not from having your ego go on the run with a fantasy. It is not critical if you lower your entropy by getting a data stream from your past life, or a past life. The manner in which you respond to this data and information is what counts more.

Do you boast and look down on others, which is a sign of insecurity, which can be traced back to a fundamental fear? Or, do you reflect on the narratives that came to you and try to learn from them? Remember, you are living in the present, not dwelling on the past.

Soul Evolution

I started to wonder a while ago, where do these Souls come from. If the Soul-learning idea holds any water, a Soul evolves through learning and understanding. The idea is then that the soul evolves from knowing little, to knowing more. And when a Soul has learned from this simulation, the Soul moves on to another simulation. This concept is akin to starting at school at a low level and gradually evolving to higher levels to finally leave the school altogether.

Assume we are in primary school now, then before primary school was kindergarten. And before kindergarten, there was a mother and father. In the same logic, after primary school will be secondary school and so forth. It is reasonable to imagine that you and me were in kindergarten before we were allowed to this primary school, right? And after we pass the tests in this primary school, we are allowed into the secondary school.

When I look at the population growth of the past two thousand years, I see a rapid rise in people entering this simulation. Here is a list:

   1st millennium (1-1000 AD): 150-300 million

   2nd millennium (1000-2000 AD): 300-600 million

   18th century (1700-1800 AD): 600-900 million

   19th century (1800-1900 AD): 900-1.6 billion

   20th century (1900-2000 AD): 1.6-6 billion

   21st century (2000-2024 AD): 6-8.2 billion

Where did those Souls come from? It makes from the LCS's perspective little sense to degrade Souls who have already passed the primary school. It makes more sense that there has been a sudden influx of so-called "young Souls" into this simulation. Young souls mean Souls with higher entropy, causing more chaos. Another way of looking at this is, Souls who, due to their lower quality, engage in high entropy behaviour. This is a camouflaged way of saying: more selfishness, more violence, more anger, more greed and so forth.

Is this a system flaw, an error, or is there another reason for this?

2.2
The Soul's Journey
Cycles, Challenges, and Transcending Memory

You may ask, "Why must the body die?" The LCS framework explains that bodies are meant to serve a specific purpose: facilitating the Soul's growth and evolution. This limited lifespan creates a sense of urgency, motivating the Soul to prioritise and achieve its goals before death. Ultimately, this drives the Soul towards either higher or lower entropy.

Causality, "if I do this, then that may happen", brings a sense of finality, promoting more thoughtful decisions. Life is shaped by factors like family, location, culture, and era. An eternal life without growth limits evolution. A new beginning provides a clean slate, free from past traumas, accomplishments, possessions, and relationships.

Moving from the Netherlands to Finland allowed me to leave behind my old history and start fresh. The new environment liberated me from feeling tied to the expectations of people in the Netherlands, who often judged me based on their perception of me. It took energy, courage and some "insanity" to break free, but it changed others' perceptions. Having said that, some people also cling onto their old perception of me, but that is their problem and not mine any more.

In the previous chapter, I explored the idea that your Soul evolves and grows over multiple lifetimes. Each lifetime contributes to your personal development, while the cumulative effect of all lifetimes shapes your Soul's evolution. Memory wiping in the LCS allows for a fresh start, free from experiences. This intentional approach ensures that every life is a new opportunity for growth, promoting continuous Soul development without the disruptions of past lives.

The Soul's Journey: A Swimming Metaphor

The Soul's journey is likened to swimming, where each stage (shallow pools to powerful ocean currents) represents a phase of growth, with unique challenges at each level. This swimming example concludes with a challenging topic: ocean currents. However, learning continues, with even more advanced levels beyond this lifetime. Each life can feel like an ultimate test, as we forget our past and future lives. To understand the need for multiple lifetimes, consider learning to swim.

As a baby, you start in shallow water, using floatation devices. You feel anxious, happy, and experience many new emotions. Despite not knowing how to swim, you have confidence.

As you progress, floatation aids are removed, and you face the fear of drowning. Surrounded by others, you realise that floating is just a lesson, not the end of your journey.

Through the various swimming courses, which are like "Life on Earth" experiences, you gain confidence. But your learning isn't over. Once you join a team, you realise that you are the slowest swimmer. Your teammates have better skills, pushing you to improve. Every advancement in the competition's hierarchy corresponds to a new stage of personal development.

One day at the beach, you see someone struggling in the waves. You swim out to help, but strong currents slow you down. This experience shows you there's more to learn beyond the pool.

Determined, you train for ocean swimming. You learn to read the waves and navigate currents, thinking you've mastered swimming. But when you jump in to save someone, you realise you're not alone —dangerous fish are nearby.

The fear of the fish, justified or not, makes you decide to go back to the safety of the indoor swimming pool. Perhaps this set-back is temporary, and you gain courage to overcome this fear. Or this set-back sets in motion a chain of fears about "things in the water" that causes a trauma or phobia.

Life can go both ways, forwards and backwards.

This journey mirrors the Soul's experiences. Like a swimmer, the Soul undergoes cycles of growth and development in various lifetimes. Every life presents opportunities to enhance qualities and abilities. Challenges such as disabilities, hardships, and obstacles help build resilience.

However, within a lifetime, memories of experiences are essential for learning and growth. Within that lifetime, you can learn from experiences, improve your responses, and adjust your emotions. Some experiences can be traumatic, and traumatic experiences can have a major impact on a lifetime. A fundamental emotion attached to this trauma is stored and processed at the Soul level. Such "quality" carries over to the next life on Earth as a challenge to address.

You may be curious as to why we don't remember the details of our previous incarnations. The Soul collects and assimilates the essential aspects of these experiences, emphasising key qualities over specific events or people. Remembering who did something to us isn't useful for the Soul's growth. Instead, the Soul is concerned with developing qualities like courage, compassion, and intuition.

Imagine an individual born and raised in a war-torn nation, constantly confronted with anxiety and danger. These experiences cultivate caution and enhance their intuition, which is crucial for survival. While recognising the enemy was useful in that lifetime, transferring that specific knowledge is not advantageous for the Soul in future incarnations.

In cases where the Soul is reborn in the same country and in similar circumstances, its character becomes more significant. Family and cultural knowledge will inform them about whom the enemy is and what to watch out for. The Soul focusses on accumulating qualities like caring for family and community, improving lives, and living with courage rather than fear.

Now imagine this Soul incarnates again in the same country and family, but relationships with former family members are different—a former sibling becomes a parent or relative. Being aware of past relationships can hinder Soul growth, potentially leading to confusion or resentment. Discarding memories of past relationships frees the Soul to focus on cultivating its essential traits, unencumbered by the baggage of old bonds or disputes.

Memory wipes between incarnations are essential for personal and spiritual growth. They liberate the Soul from the burdens of past trauma, errors, apprehension, and ties established in previous existences. Without this reset, the baggage from past lives could hinder an individual's new journey, stunting both their growth as a person and their spiritual evolution. Memory erasure offers a fresh start, liberating individuals from the past, promoting personal growth, and development.

Trauma and the Soul
Unexpected events, such as accidents, losses, or deliberate harm, are not punishments from the LCS. They may arise through the free will of others, but they can also be growth opportunities. The LCS is neutral, observing without intervention, allowing Souls to face challenges without the burden of cosmic punishment.

The Soul uses the body as an interface to engage with the world, gathering life experiences. This allows us to interact with the physical world, affecting our mental processes and bodily sensations. Our five senses act as sub-interfaces, shaping our perception of reality.

Your Soul possesses a hidden power, often neglected, known as the sixth sense. This enables you to perceive beyond the usual five senses. You can access wider truths within the LCS, such as undetectable energies, spiritual connections, and deeper levels of reality. Although everyone possesses this sixth sense, you need to develop it consciously. Your ability to perceive the interconnectedness between all beings in the LCS can develop over multiple lives, becoming a valuable tool for Soul exploration.

In a conversation with a friend, I shared an analogy to illustrate where Souls reside and how they communicate—both among themselves and with us, the participants in the virtual reality game called "Life on Earth." This story helps make abstract and unfamiliar concepts more comprehensible.

A few days before our conversation, his mother died. We had previously discussed reincarnation, the meaning of life, and dealing with life's hardships. Based on his knowledge of my views, we explored the intricacies of dying and death.

I once explained how the many coincidences in his life made sense from the LCS perspective. His intense grief and accompanying emotions in this reality were also experienced as data and information on the other side. The LCS benefited from him understanding that his mother's death was not an end, but a transition. The coincidences could be the LCS, his mother's Soul, or signals from his Soul, registered as thoughts or intuitions. They could be just a series of random events that he now wanted to make sense of. He could have chosen to respond with sadness, anger or resentment, but instead chose to see hopeful messages in those events. This deliberate act of interpretation lowered his entropy, either consciously or unconsciously.

> *Imagine that you are sitting there in Soul Land, whether you call it Heaven, an Astral Plane, or Infinity, with a VR headset and a haptic suit. Since entering the game, 'My Life on Earth', you are completely immersed in the experience. In your early years, you could still detach yourself from the game, but over time, you forgot about Soul Land.*

> *Your mother, who died during the game, has removed her VR headset and haptic suit. She can now see and communicate with your Soul, registering your emotions. She decides to guide you, saying, 'Turn left and stop at that restaurant.'*

> *While driving in the VR game, you're suddenly prompted to turn left. You spot your mum's favourite pancake restaurant and decide to stop. A sign on the wall displays her favourite proverb, which brings back fond memories. You start to believe it was a message from your mother.*

Regardless of whether it's a coincidence, truth, or exception, your response is important. You could have chosen to turn right and go to the supermarket. You listened to your intuition, which led to a comforting moment, exactly what you needed.

2.3
Collaboration, Identity, and Continuity

The Soul's journey through life and rebirth is mainly individual, but it can also involve collaboration. Souls who have met before can build on their familiarity, leading to more effective teamwork in facing life's challenges. This cooperative evolution aligns with the LCS's principles, promoting Soul collaboration to reduce entropy while preserving individuality and free will. Despite a sense of connection and shared purpose, each Soul remains an independent decision-maker. This principle respects individuality while promoting collective growth.

As I began to understand Tom's theory, I started to see the logic of the LCS. Although this may seem detached, bear with me. When someone transitions from this simulation into Soul-land, we experience sadness, followed by memories and thoughts of what might have been. These thoughts can lead to regret of all the things we could have said and done. This can serve as a learning opportunity. One lesson is to look around you and appreciate the people you have left, who are still here.

People who die quickly forget their emotional connections, as seen in Near-Death Experiences (NDE). They often describe it as waking up from a dream, just as in this world, dreams are easily forgotten. After "Life on Earth" ends, you find yourself in the afterlife. You will likely undergo a life review, debriefing, or quality assessment. Once settled, you can decide what to do next.

While you have transferred already, your loved ones are grieving, but their emotions do not affect you. You have access to their intentions, data, and information. This does not mean you are sitting there keeping a tap on those you "have left behind" though. If an intention aligns with your goals, use it. You can subtly guide someone towards a beneficial choice that benefits both of you. Both benefit from positive growth, which ensures the continuity of your Soul, and that of the LCS at large.

At the same time, you don't waste time cataloguing the intentions, data, and information of people from your previous lives. It's counterproductive, considering the number of living people who might think of you, which means you have to wait for everyone to die. They will share their intentions, data, and information. If it helps, you can act on it.

Staying behind
Grieving can be an opportunity for personal growth, even though it's painful to lose someone. I call this kind of grief "grief trauma", characterised by intense, long-lasting emotions. During this vulnerable period, you could become more open to receiving information from your LCS. The Soul who has left the game "Life on Earth" can gently suggest ideas, without violating the free will, which you receive as thoughts, intuitions, or insights.

This fragile state resembles a young, open-minded child's reception of potential past-life memories. You can also receive information from a loved one in a similar state of open-mindedness. Alternatively, you can dismiss your intuitions and insights, treating them as worthless.

The received data may be coming directly from your Soul or the Soul of your loved one. Regardless, act on the information to grow and become a better version of yourself.

Identity, Control, and the Continuity of the Self

Reincarnation offers a useful framework for grasping how the Soul continues beyond a single lifetime. It suggests that while the physical body and personality change, the Self—the union of the Soul and "you"—remains, cycling through life and death to learn, grow, and evolve. For many, this perspective is comforting, as it implies that life's challenges serve a greater purpose. However, this view of reincarnation is not without its complexities and controversies. One such complexity is the unsettling idea of a memory wipe. As discussed earlier, "you," as an instance of the Soul, loose conscious access to memories of previous incarnations.

If the Soul retains the lessons and qualities, but "you," the part of the Self experiencing life on Earth, cannot consciously access these, how can you truly grasp your purpose in life and beyond? This disconnection between lifetimes can create a sense of disintegration, where the continuity of the Self feels more abstract than tangible. If you feel attached to your current identity—your memories, relationships, and achievements—the idea that these might be erased could stir a deep fear of losing your sense of self. What remains of "you" if everything that defines your current life is forgotten in the next?

This fear becomes even more pronounced in certain interpretations of reincarnation that suggest the memory wipe is a malevolent act. Some believe that this wiping of past-life memories represents an enforced mechanism of control, not a natural part of the Soul's journey. According to these views, external forces—sometimes described as malevolent entities or systems—deliberately suppress the Soul's memories to maintain dominance over "you." In these interpretations, the Self is trapped in a cycle of reincarnation, repeatedly stripped of its knowledge and individuality, making it more vulnerable to manipulation.

This perspective often hints at the concept of "loosh", a term coined by Robert Monroe, used to describe the idea that certain non-human entities harvest emotional energy—particularly fear, pain, and suffering—from living beings. Robert, or Bob as many call him, Monroe hired Tom Campbell and Dennis Mennerich to set up the research to further study Bob's Out-of-Body experiences. This research eventually led to better understanding concepts such as Out-of-Body experience and developing techniques such as the Gateway Experience, Hemi-Sync, and the binaural beats which I will discuss later.

Similar notions of memories being wiped appear in Gnostic beliefs, which say that the archons, malevolent entities created by the demiurge, trap souls in the material world. By stripping souls of divine knowledge and perpetuating cycles of suffering, the archons maintain their control. The Alien Abduction Hypothesis offers another parallel, where some interpretations suggest extraterrestrial beings manipulate human memories, erasing or altering them to conceal their influence and sustain their experiments. These so-called aliens would not interfere with the reincarnation process perhaps, but the mechanism of erasing memory is a common theme in that narrative.

How about these Gnostic wipes are real, but not for the malevolent reason as proposed? Perhaps the early Gnostics discovered the actuality of these wipes, but not understood or wanted to see the beneficial side? Or our interpretation of their texts are not accurate?

Furthermore, Jerry Marzinski's ideas on demonic possession align with these themes. Jerry Marzinski worked for decades at various mental health institutions in the USA as a therapist. He suggests that conditions such as schizophrenia may serve as a gateway for third-party entities—what he describes as malevolent beings or "demons"—to inhabit the mind. These entities, he argues, influence thoughts, emotions, and behaviours, erasing or distorting the individual's sense of self, and perpetuating confusion and suffering. Marzinski observed and documented the possessions, sometimes multiple identities in one person, of his patients or clients. These people, his patients, were hospitalised due to various reasons, often to do with violence.

But what about those people, how can better control or manage these "voices in the head" and sudden urges?

Beyond metaphysical theories, real-world entities—such as the media, political systems, religions, ideologies, and other societal structures—can perpetuate fear, division, and ignorance to maintain control. A significant method of this control involves the deliberate rewriting or erasure of history, encapsulated in the phrase "victors rewrite history." By reshaping collective memory, these forces distort the understanding of the past, suppress alternative narratives, and reinforce their authority. Similarly, the media and political institutions typically spread narratives of fear and uncertainty, while religions and ideologies may exploit existential anxieties to assert dominance and suppress dissent.

Within these frameworks, the memory wipe—whether literal, as in reincarnation theories, or metaphorical, as in the manipulation of history and information—serves a sinister purpose. These forces keep "you" unaware of the true nature of the Self, its experiences, and its potential, ensuring a steady supply of emotional energy, compliance, or distraction through the struggles of each new life. While such theories remain speculative, they resonate with a deep-seated fear of external control and the erosion of personal autonomy.

However, embracing such theories, particularly the idea of a memory wipe as a malevolent act, presents a crucial choice: Will you let this belief drive your behaviour through fear, or will you use it as an opportunity to grow? Acting out of fear—whether through passivity, rebellion, or nihilism—ultimately feeds into the very cycles of control and entropy these theories describe. Fear-based responses can lead to passivity, where individuals feel helpless against external forces, or to misplaced blame, deflecting responsibility and undermining the agency required for meaningful growth.

Overcoming Fear

Instead, we can transform fear into a tool for lowering entropy and nurturing growth within the Larger Consciousness System. This transformation begins with reframing the challenge. If one views the memory wipe—or any perceived external control—not as a barrier but as a motivation for learning, the focus shifts to the present moment and the choices available within it. By confronting fear and acting with clarity and purpose, "you" can reclaim agency and contribute to the evolution of the Self and the LCS.

The fear of losing one's identity—whether through the natural processes of reincarnation or the imagined machinations of external forces—reflects a more profound uncertainty about the Self and its continuity. It flourishes in the unknown, feeding on the gaps where understanding fails. However, we can avoid this fear. By reframing reincarnation as an opportunity for growth and focusing on the present moment, you can reclaim your sense of agency. The journey of the Self is not defined by what is forgotten, but by what is learned and how those lessons are applied. Letting go of fear, particularly the fear of losing one's identity, is a crucial step towards embracing the challenges and opportunities of this life with clarity and purpose. In this way, fear becomes a catalyst for reducing entropy and aligning with the greater purpose of the LCS, rather than an obstacle that perpetuates cycles of suffering.

That your memory is disconnected, or rather fades, after your birth I consider a truth. So, in a way, the memory wipes concept is real, but not as a punishment, evil deed or necessity for an alien intervention only. To remember all your past-life experiences probably will hold you back anyway. The most important logical reason to me that we forget our past-life experiences is that, the Soul encompasses the core qualities of you. These core qualities you bring with you into a new life experience. As such, every new life experience throws you back onto your core qualities and there is no to little chance to act based on what you have learned from a pervious life experience.

For example, if you would remember the ways to manipulate and influence others as to get quicker what you want in life, you would be very tempted to start using this. Even though this sounds great at first, you will miss the opportunities to discover new or better ways of achieving your goals. You would stay stuck in old patterns with little room to evolve and grow. Furthermore, the temptation to focus on possessions to gain status, admiration, and wealth leads you toward an existence of thinking about yourself, and less of the well-being of the others. In other words, chances are you de-evolve rather than evolve, according to the logic of the LCS.

In a later chapter, I delve into this idea of shortcuts to get what you want, including the consequences of such behaviour. And this is not only about gathering "stuff" but also about gathering spiritual trinkets to boost your ego and gain status within a community. My focus is on improving the quality of my Soul instead. I accept the memory wipe and imagine how in a next life experience I could have a better start. What core qualities should I improve upon now?

3
Forces
Order and Chaos

You can't hone a blade on velvet.

Love and fear are opposites on a fundamental spectrum, which I call "spectrum-duality". This duality creates a dynamic space for Consciousness, allowing souls to reduce entropy by choosing love or increase it by choosing fear. The LCS, which is neutral, driven by a desire for experience, evolves and expands by reducing entropy. If its quality decreases, leading to increased entropy (chaos), the system will eventually cease to exist.

The LCS faces a dilemma. It must have experiences to continue to exist, but it cannot force these experiences onto the Soul. They would lack authenticity, as they would not arise from the Soul's free will. The LCS at first would have a Soul enter random circumstances in for example the simulation, "Life on Earth", just to get an extensive number of experiences. After experiencing many lifetimes, it makes sense for the LCS to let the Soul decide its life missions. At some point, the Soul knows what to pick from in order to more effectively create the needed experiences.

> *Bear in mind, there are many other simulations with very different dynamics and growth (decline) opportunities. Even inside this physicalism oriented simulation, our Universe, are possibly very many planets and solar systems where the Soul can experience a form of life.*

The Soul cannot foresee its next life's details. While some broad concepts regarding "Earthly Life" remain constant, such as seasons, laws of nature, circumstances such as culture, technology, and beliefs can undergo significant changes. With many unknown factors, accurately predicting one's future existence on Earth is unfeasible. Some other learning (experience) environments and situations nurture the Soul with gentleness and love, demonstrating their positive impact on growth. Others provide opportunities for the Soul to cultivate different traits. Consider "Life on Earth" as a tough class to be in.

In low-entropy situations, the Soul is more productive and fulfilled, leading to longer and more enjoyable lives. Conversely, high-entropy environments are often characterised by anger and violence, resulting, on average, in shorter lifespans and greater suffering. The LCS only needs to provide a range of experience environments, allowing Souls to make their own choices and experiences. The Soul's desire for longer, more fulfilling lives drives it towards low-entropy states, which maximise rewards and positive experiences. This self-interest guides the LCS towards a path of increased love.

Thus, the Soul learns over time that low entropy states result in a more fulfilling and longer life. Though, do not confuse lower entropy (loving) with naivety and passivity. Each Soul moves through environments without direct guidance from the LCS, but their collective experiences shape it. By experiencing love-rich and fear-intense environments, your Soul expands its Consciousness, enriching the LCS. The more Souls succumb to forces that encourage fear, the more chaotic, high-entropy, the LCS becomes.

The Duality of Love and Fear.

Both extremes of love and fear are necessary for Soul development. Choosing between love and fear allows you to make significant decisions that affect their quality. This dynamic interaction creates an environment where your Soul's evolution is shaped by your conscious choices, actively reducing or increasing its entropy. Through this process, each Soul's journey adds to your and the collective quality of the LCS, positioning choice-driven evolution as central to its design.

This chapter examines the underlying influences that shape our thoughts, actions, and experiences. I explore the impact of fear on behaviour, the balance between Good and Evil, and the duality of virtues and vices. Recognising these forces can help you understand what motivates your decisions and the external factors that may influence them.

Anatomy of Fear
In "The Anatomy of Fear," I explain how various levels of fear stem from our fundamental survival instincts. The lowest level is primal, focussed on physical safety and evading danger. Higher levels are more complex and introspective, dealing with social acceptance and existential questions.

In "The Anatomy of Good and Evil," I explore moral behaviour as a continuum, not a binary. Actions can range from respecting others' autonomy to infringing on it for personal gain or power. Individuals frequently rationalise harmful conduct as necessary for self-defence or the common good.

People may rationalise unethical behaviour as protective, leading to harmful actions. Power imbalances can distort ethical judgement, making it easier to slide towards harm without consequences. Understanding how justifications blur moral lines is crucial, particularly in situations of unequal power.

Virtues and Vices
In "Virtues and Vices", I examine the nuanced nature of virtues and vices. They exist on a continuum, not as black-and-white opposites. For example, traits such as lust and chastity, or greed and charity, have varying degrees of positivity and negativity.

Greed, when moderated, can lead to admirable ambition, driving one to achieve great things. However, if left unchecked, it can lead to selfishness and dissatisfaction. This section provides a structured approach for understanding the pros and cons of each trait, empowering individuals to make informed choices that align with their authentic selves.

Shame, Blame, and Guilt
The chapter discusses how emotions play a dual role in shaping personal growth and relationships. When balanced, they promote self-reflection, accountability, and learning. Imbalance, however, leads to self-loathing, resentment, and emotional burnout, impeding progress. It also examines the impact of emotions like shame, blame, and guilt on self-discovery and personal growth. By recognising and striking a balance between these emotions, individuals can use them as tools for self-development and healthy relationships. The following chapter will explore how daily decisions shape character and personal journeys.

Spectrum Duality

I introduce the concept of "Spectrum-Duality", which proposes that love and fear exist at opposite ends of a wide spectrum. This concept highlights the idea that growth can occur through both gradual, incremental changes and sudden, transformative shifts. This framework provides adaptability, permitting gradual advancement without the need for an all-or-nothing approach to personal growth.

However, growth does not always happen gradually. Spectrum-duality recognises pivotal points—significant life events, profound insights, or intense experiences—that can suddenly change a person's position on the spectrum. These unanticipated events can propel a person towards greater authenticity or prompt them to confront hidden aspects of their identity. Spectrum-duality captures the idea that most change happens gradually, but pivotal moments can catalyse rapid transformation, shifting one's perspective and altering their trajectory.

When you read through the next chapters about these forces, you will see how they are intertwined with various descriptions of fear.

Fears

The concept of fear is central to understanding the operation of the LCS. This book aims to shed light on the meaning of fear and provide an overview of how different types of fears relate to each other. To do so, I have created a hierarchy of fear. This framework will guide you in recognising your fears as we delve into the concepts of authenticity and measuring progress. Keep in mind that the hierarchy is not rigid, as there is a natural overlap between categories.

This hierarchy illustrates the structure of fear, showing how each level builds on more fundamental concerns. The foundation consists of primal fears, such as physical pain and suffering, and fear of death and non-existence. As we climb higher, these fears evolve into more complex, abstract worries, but they remain connected to the underlying fears below. Each tier represents a distinct form of vulnerability, whether it's physical, social, or existential.

The hierarchical structure of fears shows that they evolve alongside human needs. For instance, the fear of rejection arises from the desire to conform to societal norms. As fears become more abstract, they reflect our quest for identity, meaning, and a sense of belonging.

This progression reveals that deeper-rooted fears, such as those concerning life's purpose, stem from fundamental survival anxieties. For example, a fear of insignificance can result in existential loneliness, mirroring the fear of physical separation. Thus, these levels are interconnected, with each one amplifying or reaffirming the ones below.

The Anatomy of Fear

I came to the idea of making a lookup table of various kinds of fears, as often people say they do not have any fears. That is okay, but after a short conversation, the first descriptions of possible fears begin to emerge. The idea of having a fear seems to be something to feel ashamed about. Over time, I developed an understanding of how fears could be organised as to show the relationships between fears, and how certain fears are based on other fears. The hierarchy organises our fears into categories, from immediate physical threats to existential questions, helping us understand the complexities of human vulnerability.

1. Primitive/Fundamental Fears:

These are the most basic instincts related to survival and physical well-being.

Physical Pain and Suffering:
The body's instinct to avoid harm and discomfort.

Death or Non-existence:
The ultimate fear, reflecting an individual's desire to preserve life.

2. Survival-Related Fears:

These fears extend beyond physical survival, requiring support from others.

Abandonment:
The fear of being left alone, leading to exposure to dangers that one cannot handle alone.

Isolation:
The fear of being disconnected from social ties, causing feelings of vulnerability and isolation.

Dependence on Others:
Fear of relying on others for survival, with worries about their reliability.

Instability and Insecurity:
Fear of losing a stable and safe environment, leading to uncertainty and risk.

Isolation from collective assets:
Anxiety about not having access to shared resources, potentially affecting well-being and support.

Declining confidence in caregivers:
Fear that those responsible for crucial care, like loved ones, may fail or deceive, exposing one to harm.

3. Social and Relational Fears:

These concerns involve how others perceive and value us, as well as our desire for acceptance.

Rejection and Unworthiness:
Fear of being rejected due to personal flaws.

Social Judgement:
Fear of criticism and social rejection, impacting one's social status.

Loss of Identity:
Fear of losing significance within a group, leading to disconnection and invisibility.

Betrayal:
Concern about close relationships ending in betrayal, eroding emotional security and trust.

Unmet Expectations:
Fear of failing to meet societal expectations, such as in family or work, leading to rejection.

Social Status:
Fear of losing respect, leading to isolation.

4. Existential and Identity-Based Fears:

These fears concern a person's place and purpose in the world, addressing more in-depth questions of identity, meaning, and connection.

Loss of Purpose and Meaning:
Fear that life may lack purpose, leading to a profound sense of disconnection.

Fear of Insignificance:
Anxiety that one's life or actions has no broader meaning, creating a sense of isolation for a larger purpose.

Fear of being unseen or misunderstood:
Concern about not being fully known or appreciated, causing deep loneliness.

Loss of authenticity:
Fear that one's identity or actions lack genuineness, leading to self-alienation and disconnection.

Fear of legacy and impact:
Worry that one's life has no lasting value, resulting in a sense of futility.

Fear of Profound Disconnection:
Fear of fundamental separation from others or a larger whole, leading to existential abandonment.

Fear of Failing Self-Actualisation:
Concern over not achieving one's full potential, causing a sense of meaninglessness.

Fear of Exposing the True Self:
Anxiety about revealing inner thoughts and feelings, leading to fear of misunderstanding or rejection, exacerbating isolation.

This structure shows a hierarchy of fears, starting with basic survival instincts and progressing to existential concerns. Each level builds on the previous one, highlighting the interconnectedness of survival, identity, social connections, and purpose.

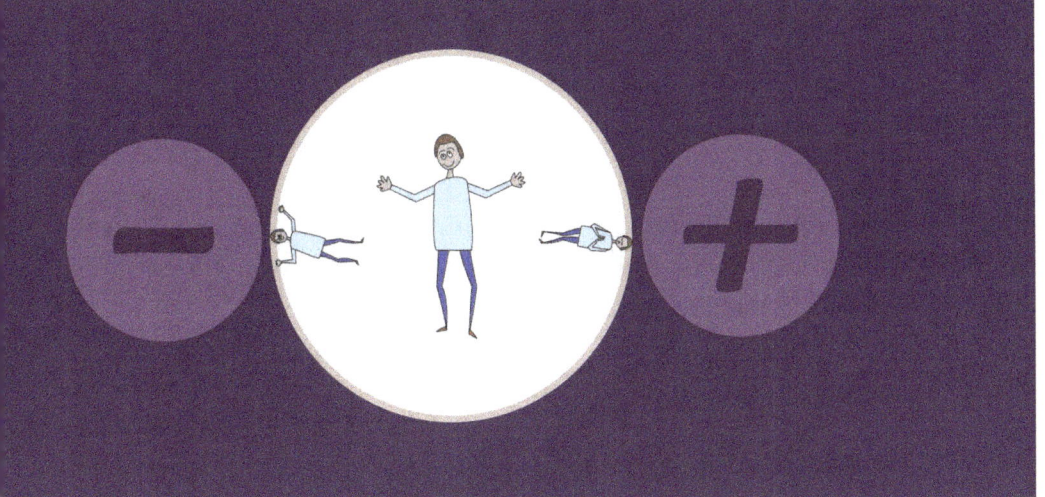

3.1

Good and Evil

A Spectrum-Duality with Justifications for Evil

This framework examines Good and Evil as motivating factors in human behaviour, starting from higher moral principles and moving down to the most basic survival needs. Higher moral principles serve to justify loving behaviour, and also to create fear. In each category that I propose, you find how Good and Evil, love and fear, hide behind on the surface, recognisable narratives. The danger is in blindly accepting a narrative without questioning its underlying motives or examining the eventual outcomes. If these motives and results were positive and reduced disorder, few would object. However, often, deceptive slogans and ideologies mask malicious agendas.

To understand Evil, it is essential to consider the ways people justify harmful actions. In numerous instances, justifications rest on ideas of self-preservation, security, or a sense of higher purpose. However, these reasons can quickly move from legitimate defence to pre-emptive strikes and coercion, sliding along the spectrum from morally neutral acts to true harm and cruelty. This shift becomes particularly dangerous when there is a power imbalance—when one side has the strength to act with minimal risk and little accountability.

Justifying Evil Acts

People regularly justify morally questionable actions, such as self-defence or defending values, even if it means harming others. This is particularly true in situations of power imbalance, where those with more power regularly view the less powerful as threats, obstacles, or simply as a means to an end. Power can distort ethical judgement, making people think that harmful actions are justifiable if they can be carried out without consequences.

Self-Defence vs Pre-emptive Justification

People view self-defence as a morally neutral act, as it aims to protect one's life or safety without intending to cause unnecessary harm. However, pre-emptive actions complicate this neutrality. When someone reacts to a speculative or imagined threat, they enter morally ambiguous territory. In a pre-emptive mindset, one justifies harm without a real or immediate threat, placing them closer to the Evil side of the spectrum.

In cases of power imbalance, this justification becomes even more dangerous. The more powerful side may feel justified in acting "just in case" to prevent potential threats from the weaker side, often disregarding their autonomy. Such pre-emptive actions lead to control and harm without resistance, pushing moral boundaries with minimal accountability.

The "Greater Good" and Sacrificial Justifications

Another common justification for Evil is the belief that harm is essential for the "greater good." In such cases, actions are portrayed as sacrifices made for security, order, or moral ideals, disregarding the free will of those affected. When power imbalances exist, the powerful may feel entitled to decide what they deem "best" for everyone, rationalising actions that violate the autonomy of the less powerful. By framing choices as essential for a larger purpose, they overlook the impact on individuals' rights and freedom, treating them as obstacles rather than recognising them as independent beings with their needs.

In this way, power becomes a tool for overriding moral restraint. Those who hold significant power feel entitled to make decisions that harm others in the belief that their vision of the "greater good" justifies it. Such reasoning suppresses empathy and supports the exploitation of those who cannot resist.

Lack of Accountability and Moral Distance

With a significant power imbalance comes a lack of accountability and a resulting moral distance. When individuals or groups hold substantial power, they can avoid consequences for harmful actions. This reduces their sense of responsibility, creating emotional distance from the impact of their actions on those less powerful. They may justify their actions as "unavoidable" or even dismiss the consequences entirely, given the lack of opposition or repercussions.

This moral distance makes it easier to dehumanise others, viewing them as lesser or irrelevant to broader goals. As this dehumanisation continues, the powerful may justify increasingly harmful actions as necessary or inconsequential, effectively placing themselves outside the moral limits that normally govern interactions between equals.

The Anatomy of Good and Evil—a Structure

This framework of "Good and Evil" outlines five levels through which human motivations and moral choices develop and evolve. Good and Evil are not rigid or simple opposites but represent areas along a continuum, which this text refers to as spectrum-duality. Most actions and intentions fall somewhere along this spectrum, rarely being purely "good" or "Evil" and often involving a mix of growth and stagnation, empathy and self-interest, or freedom and control.

Good and Evil are abstract concepts that have a profound impact on individual choices, relationships, and societal systems. To understand their complexities, it's helpful to break them down into aspects, revealing how they operate at various levels of human behaviour. This method helps us understand Good and Evil as dynamic forces influenced by motivations, values, and power. It allows us to examine their manifestation in everyday life and explore the reasons behind people's actions.

My model has its limits, since reality is far more complex, with exceptions, deviations, intricacies, and countless other factors. Categorising things as either Good or bad is challenging, given the complexity of life. However, I still do it because these concepts provide you with something to think about when you do the Authenticity exercises. Consider this outline on the subjects of Good and Evil, and contemplate how these concepts align with the fears I have outlined and the virtues, vices and other human qualities that I explore in the following chapters.

The Anatomy

Title:
Defines the realm where Good and Evil operate, providing a lens for examining their manifestations, moral implications, and power dynamics.

Core Idea:
The essence of Good and Evil at an interaction level.

Human Expression:
The intention behind people's actions and choices.

Power dynamics:
How power affects these forces, especially in relationships and systems.

Transcendent Good and Profound Evil

Core Idea:
Good and Evil are powerful forces that profoundly shape society. Transcendent Good values autonomy and promotes collective harmony, while profound Evil justifies harm in the name of progress or control, disregarding people's rights.

Human Expression:
Positive: Actions that promote growth, equality, and respect for all living beings.
Negative: Large-scale harm that is justified as necessary for order, progress, or security.

Power Dynamics:
Individuals in positions of authority often justify their actions, even if they are harmful, as necessary for maintaining control or serving a "higher purpose". This frequently results in widespread suffering, as the powerful disregard the autonomy and well-being of the less powerful.

Moral Ideals and Values

Core Idea:
Moral principles shape behaviour, going beyond self-interest to embrace principles such as fairness, honesty, and selflessness. These can motivate noble actions or be perverted for selfish gain.

Human expression:
Positive: applying values fairly, respecting autonomy and fairness for everyone.

Negative: harming others to enforce one's vision of justice, frequently targeting those deemed unworthy or opposing ideals.

Power Dynamics:
Imbalances in power can make actions that are motivated by values seem righteous, but they frequently mask the oppression of those deemed inferior. Leaders or groups may impose their ideals, disregarding others' autonomy under the guise of morality.

Empathy and Social Connection

Core Idea:
Empathy and relationships create moral obligations to consider others' experiences. Suppressing empathy allows people to rationalise harm, treating others as expendable.

Human expression:
Positive: Actions are motivated by empathy, respecting the needs and autonomy of others.

Negative: Harm justifies itself by disregarding empathy and often portrays others as unworthy or inferior.

Power Dynamics:
Those in power can use moral distance to dismiss the vulnerable, rationalising harm or exploitation as a necessity. This creates habitual neglect of empathy, enabling systematic abuse.

Desire for Control and Influence

Core Idea:
The pursuit of control shapes relationships and environments. When control infringes on others' freedom, it crosses moral boundaries.

Human expression:
Positive: Working together to exert collaborative control, respecting others' autonomy.

Negative: Exerting dominance by assuming others might act against one's interests, leading to oppressive pre-emptive control.

Power Dynamics:
Imbalanced power typically leads to unchecked dominance, where those in control impose their will under the pretext of maintaining order and limiting others' freedom for their gain.

Foundational Drives

Core Idea:
Basic survival instincts are morally neutral; it can evolve into intricate justifications for causing harm. Balancing self-interest and the welfare of others is a delicate act.

Human expression:
Positive: Striking a balance between self-preservation and recognition of mutual needs and autonomy.

Negative: Pre-emptive harm, rationalised as necessary for survival, even in response to perceived threats.

Power Dynamics:
Those who are in power can use their advantage to justify oppressive actions by framing them as necessary for "security", and then exploit that narrative to suppress others.

These layers show how justifications for Evil typically rest on distorted views of self-defence, greater good, and power. Those with significant power justify actions they might otherwise avoid if they saw others as equals. The result is a gradual slide along the spectrum-duality, from morally neutral or defensible actions to justifications for exploitation and harm, especially when power enables these actions to go unchallenged.

The Morality of Evil

Good and Evil, as I place them within the framework of the LCS, are not fixed absolutes but dynamic points on a spectrum. The interactions and choices made within this spectrum form the foundation for learning and growth in the simulation "Life on Earth". The LCS's ultimate purpose is to nurture evolution through the reduction of entropy, and as we navigate this simulation, the spectrum-duality between Good and Evil provides a fertile ground for understanding the consequences of our actions and intentions. In this section, we will examine how the progression from passive to active participation in Evil reflects personal and collective growth, emphasising the need for conscious decision-making rather than reliance on ignorance.

Passive to Active Complicity
One of the most pressing moral questions is whether the severity of Evil lies in its conception or its execution. Is it more destructive to imagine, instigate, promote, enable, or directly carry out an act of Evil? Each step represents an escalation of intent and action, and together, they create a chain that facilitates harm.

Take war, for example. A conflict begins with the imagining of conquest or destruction, followed by the planning and promotion of such an agenda. Financiers, logisticians, and enablers step in to resource the effort, often hiding behind bureaucratic processes or profit-driven motives. Finally, soldiers and operatives carry out the act itself—war's physical expression. While the media points the attention to the visible brutality of war, it pays little attention to those who quietly support or enable it. Yet without the backing of enablers, the act might never materialise.

Complicity in Evil exists on a spectrum, from passive condoning to active participation. Passive complicity typically manifests as indirect benefits, such as profiting from resources obtained through war. For example, a society may enjoy the influx of cheap energy after a conflict, yet few pause to question the origins of this abundance. Ignorance typically serves as a defence, but how long can one remain unaware of the origins of such gains? The moral question intensifies when an individual knows about the origins but chooses to act—or not act—accordingly.

Active complicity, on the other hand, involves deliberate actions such as financing, enabling, or promoting harm. The transition from passive to active complicity can be imperceptible and gradual. A person might begin by "looking the other way," then progress to condoning harmful actions, and finally become a direct enabler or participant. This progression highlights the need for reflection and awareness. Where does one's responsibility begin, and at what point does inaction become indistinguishable from action?

The Role of Nepotism in Facilitating Evil

Another mechanism that facilitates Evil is nepotism. Small groups within a society can consolidate power and control by favouring like-minded individuals who share their goals or ideologies. This selective favouring often comes with an unspoken agreement: those who benefit from nepotism must look the other way when questionable actions arise, or provide public support when the time arises. For example, a business leader may favour loyal associates for promotions, knowing that these individuals will support unethical decisions in the future. Similarly, political elites may use nepotism to ensure complicity within their ranks, creating a network of mutual dependence that perpetuates harm.

Nepotism thrives on silence and complicity, as those who benefit fear losing their privileges. This dynamic facilitates the execution of harmful actions and shields those in power from accountability. Over time, the normalisation of such practices erodes societal integrity, making it increasingly difficult for individuals to distinguish passive acceptance from active participation in systemic Evil.

If nepotism thrives on voluntary compliance, emotional and physical blackmail gives people a much more direct choice: go along with the plan, or suffer. Whether this involves a real choice remains unclear. One has the obligation to keep the vessel, the body, alive and functional. The consequences of such a choice remain the important question. How can you navigate this complicated situation in such a way that you still lower your entropy and not jeopardise your livelihood or that of your loved ones?

It comes back to controlling your intentions, emotions, thoughts, words, and actions. Each attribute and transition from one attribute to the other offers you the chance to stay as closely aligned with your Soul. If you are asked to say certain things that support Evil, make sure you set a clear and loving intention in advance. Work on your emotions so that you do not spread Evil, feel or imagine love for the possible victims. I can understand this sounds like a mind trick to escape your responsibility. Considering the life-threatening situation and assuming you want to keep your body and that of your loved ones alive, I see this as the best approach.

As with much in this book, reality falls short of a binary opposition, and the above two examples represent extreme cases of nepotism: voluntary and forced compliance. You can choose, although the situation sometimes seems bleak and hopeless. Do as well as you can do.

The Emotional Middle Ground

Complicity in Evil often arises not from ignorance or direct coercion, but from the complex emotional dynamics that operate between these extremes. Fear of shame, ridicule, or guilt can lead people to comply, remain silent, or even participate in acts that they know to be wrong. These emotions, though uncomfortable, are powerful tools, often manipulated to ensure compliance.

> *Imagine a scenario at a party where inappropriate behaviour unfolds—perhaps someone in a position of influence harasses another guest. You see this happening, and your immediate emotional response is a mix of discomfort and fear: fear of speaking up and being ostracised, fear of becoming a target yourself, or fear of losing your standing within the group. Rationalisations quickly follow, such as "It's not my place to intervene" or "Someone else will surely address this." Yet, each choice you make in such a situation reflects your inner alignment with love or fear, and eventually with your Soul.*

Choosing love over fear takes immense courage. Speaking up, resisting, or refusing to cooperate may lead to personal discomfort or even significant consequences, but it also nurtures growth within the LCS framework. By aligning your intentions with love and compassion, you contribute to lowering entropy in the larger Consciousness system. In this sense, every act of courage—no matter how small—is a step toward personal and collective evolution.

Personal growth emerges from these moments of moral clarity. When you decide to act out of love—whether by defending someone, refusing to participate in harmful actions, or speaking up—you set a precedent for others to follow. Courage spreads, and small acts of resistance can inspire larger waves of change. Moreover, by consciously managing your emotions, you ensure that your actions remain aligned with the principles of growth and entropy reduction. Recognising fear, guilt, or shame as opportunities for growth rather than obstacles helps you navigate the complexities of moral decision-making.

In these emotionally charged scenarios, the line between passive and active complicity becomes blurred. A single decision to stay silent may seem minor, but over time, repeated inaction erodes integrity and strengthens systemic harm. Conversely, even small acts of resistance can shift the dynamic, demonstrating the power of intentional, love-driven choices in the simulation of "Life on Earth."

Connecting to the Learning Process of the LCS
Emotions play a significant role in how we justify or avoid accountability. Guilt and fear often prevent people from confronting the consequences of their actions or inactions. For example, the sight of suffering may evoke discomfort, leading some to look away rather than engage. Others, driven by apathy or even enjoyment of harm, may choose to participate actively in perpetuating suffering.

Understanding and managing these emotions are crucial to making conscious moral decisions. Avoiding guilt by rationalising or ignoring harm only deepens one's complicity. Conversely, facing discomfort with courage can lead to growth and a higher moral standard.

Repetition and intensity magnify the moral consequences of our choices. A single act of negligence may seem insignificant, but repeated over time, it becomes a pattern that shapes one's character and impacts the collective whole. Similarly, the intensity of an action amplifies its effect, whether Good or Evil. Financing a single act of harm might seem minor, but continuously enabling systemic exploitation compounds the moral weight.

Within the LCS, each choice, either passive or active, contributes to the larger process of growth and learning. Complicity, in all its forms, provides an opportunity for reflection and change. By recognising the progression from passive to active involvement in Evil and addressing the emotional and habitual forces at play, individuals can make deliberate choices that align with the LCS's goal of reducing entropy.

The journey from ignorance to awareness, and from avoidance to accountability, concerns more than just personal morality; it involves contributing to the evolution of the collective Consciousness. The spectrum of Good and Evil serves as a tool for learning. How we navigate it defines our growth within the simulation.

3.2
Virtues and Vices
Forces of Virtue and Vice: A Dual Perspective

This chapter examines virtues and vices as intricate parts of human nature, capable of shaping your life positively or negatively. These characteristics exist on a spectrum, influenced by internal motivations and beliefs, as well as external factors. The chapter presents a concise table, serving as a reference for understanding the double-sided nature of each trait.

I present two frameworks: the traditional Seven Deadly Sins and Virtues, and modern emotions like shame, resentment, and guilt. These familiar lenses offer recognisable ways to examine core human traits. However, they are not exhaustive; the same ideas can be framed differently or adapted for different viewpoints. This serves as a guide to consider the positive and negative aspects of virtues and vices.

This framework suggests that human traits form a bell curve, with most people in the middle and only a few at the extremes. Stability is maintained when individuals occupy this central position. However, external factors can cause individuals to move towards one extreme, which affects society. In times of imbalance, society can either devolve into chaos or evolve towards a more harmonious state. This highlights the significance of making thoughtful, well-balanced decisions.

As a Soul, making authentic choices requires distinguishing between internal values and external influences shaping thoughts and behaviour. It's a gradual process, spanning multiple lifetimes, where every choice offers an opportunity to practise virtue. Progress isn't always linear, with setbacks possible. This continuous process is crucial for personal growth, self-discovery, and making independent decisions aligned with your values, not impulsive reactions to external influences.

Cardinal Sins and Virtues

The Seven Cardinal Sins—Lust, Gluttony, Greed, Sloth, Wrath, Envy, and Pride—are traditionally viewed as sources of moral failure. However, each sin has a flip side: a virtue that channels its energy constructively. This section pairs each sin with its corresponding virtue, showing how, when balanced, these qualities stimulate growth rather than degradation.

For example, Chastity can transform Lust into deep respect for relationships, while Patience can turn Wrath into a force for positive change. However, just like vices, virtues can also become excessive, hindering growth. This viewpoint highlights the importance of moderation and balance in all aspects of life. Carefully considering both pros and cons can help find a balanced and authentic expression of oneself.

The Lookup Table

Anatomy of the Lookup Table
This lookup table provides a structured overview of essential human emotions and traits, highlighting their benefits and limitations. Each entry follows a consistent format, making it easy to understand and engage with. The entries include:

> **Title:**
> The concept's title provides a clear identifier.
>
> **Definition:**
> A concise explanation of the concept's essential features and importance.

Description:
A detailed examination of the concept, including its functions, impacts, and practical applications, with examples.

Threshold:
The point where the concept stops being beneficial or manageable and becomes harmful or overwhelming. This highlights its limitations and potential risks.

Lust

Definition:
A strong desire, typically physical or emotional, that drives connection and exploration but needs boundaries to maintain respect and fulfilment.

Description:
When managed well, lust inspires creativity and connection. It stays healthy when guided by respect for yourself and others, allowing curiosity without crossing ethical lines or personal limits. For example, feeling attracted to someone can lead to a meaningful relationship when approached with care. However, unchecked lust can lead to impulsive actions and emotional distance, causing objectification and even addiction.

Threshold:
Impatience marks the tipping point for lust. When desire becomes urgent or impatient, it overrides respect and consideration, turning connection into possession. This impatience pushes you towards impulsive actions that ignore boundaries and can lead to treating others as objects rather than people.

Chastity

Definition:
Practising self-control in relationships, channelling desire into meaningful affection while respecting personal values.

Description:
Chastity directs lust into respectful, caring relationships by emphasising restraint. This moderation strengthens self-respect and cultivates genuine intimacy. For instance,

choosing to wait before deepening a relationship can build a stronger emotional connection. However, excessive chastity may suppress natural desires, creating shame around normal feelings and leading to an aversion to intimacy.

Threshold:
Chastity's tipping point is the fear of vulnerability. When the desire for control becomes a shield against closeness, chastity turns into avoidance. This fear creates shame around natural desires, breeding judgement and guilt, and leading to emotional distance.

Gluttony

Definition:
Overindulging in pleasures like food or comfort, which can weaken self-control and gratitude.

Description:
Enjoying life's pleasures, such as good food or relaxation, can promote gratitude when done mindfully. Healthy enjoyment means appreciating these pleasures without going overboard. For example, savouring a delicious meal brings joy. But overindulgence weakens self-control, leading to dependency and a loss of appreciation for moderation.

Threshold:
Insatiability marks the tipping point for gluttony. When seeking pleasure loses its limits, the joy in simple things fades, and indulgence becomes neediness. This insatiability breeds dependency and greed, disconnecting you from gratitude.

Temperance

Definition:
Practising moderation, allowing enjoyment within limits to create balance and inner harmony.

Description:
Temperance guides indulgence by encouraging self-respect and moderation, letting you enjoy life's pleasures without excess. For example, eating a small piece of cake can be part of a balanced lifestyle. However, excessive temperance can lead to rigid self-denial, detaching you from pleasure and creating a restrictive attitude towards life's joys.

Threshold:
Rigidity marks the tipping point for temperance. When moderation becomes inflexible, it cuts you off from joy and spontaneity. Pleasure turns into something to control or avoid. This rigidity leads to a joyless existence, causing unnecessary restraint.

Greed

Definition:
An excessive desire for more than you need, which can drive ambition but may lead to selfishness and dissatisfaction.

Description:
When managed properly, this drive inspires growth and care for loved ones. Greed remains positive when it benefits both you and others. For example, working hard to provide for your family deserves commendation. But taken too far, greed leads to isolation and dissatisfaction, eroding integrity and connections.

Threshold:
Greed reaches its tipping point with insecurity. When fear of not having enough drives ambition, your self-worth becomes tied to material success, creating a need to hoard or overreach. This insecurity leads to isolation, dissatisfaction, and disconnection from others.

Charity

Definition:
Voluntarily offering help or resources to others, balanced by self-care to avoid enabling dependency.

Description:
Charity counters greed by promoting empathy and generosity, enriching both the giver and the receiver. Practised healthily, it involves boundaries that preserve your well-being. For example, helping a friend in need while caring for yourself creates respect. Yet, in excess, charity can lead to burnout, creating dependency and preventing others from growing.

Threshold:
Self-neglect represents the tipping point for charity. When helping others become your sole source of worth, you might ignore your needs, leading to self-sacrifice without balance. This self-neglect creates burnout and enables dependency, hindering genuine growth for everyone involved.

Sloth

Definition:
Avoiding effort or activity, which can provide rest but, in excess, leads to stagnation and neglect of responsibilities.

Description:
Balanced rest allows necessary rejuvenation, refreshing your mind without promoting apathy. Taking a day off to relax can boost your energy. However, taken too far, sloth leads to procrastination and avoidance, causing dissatisfaction and neglect of important tasks.

Threshold:
Sloth's tipping point is avoidance. When rest becomes a way to evade responsibility, relaxation turns into apathy. This avoidance breeds procrastination and self-sabotage, leaving tasks undone and goals unachieved.

Diligence

Definition:
A persistent commitment to effort and purpose, encouraging productivity while respecting the need for rest.

Description:
Diligence brings structure to life, enabling resilience and accomplishment. When balanced, it promotes a healthy mix of productivity and well-being. For example, consistently working towards a goal while allowing time for rest leads to sustainable success. In excess, though, diligence can result in workaholism and burnout, causing emotional distance and neglect of personal needs.

Threshold:
Perfectionism represents the tipping point for diligence. When diligence becomes a quest for flawless performance, it fuels an unrelenting drive that drains all joy. This

perfectionism creates workaholism, leading to burnout and detachment from personal needs and relationships.

Wrath

Definition:
Intense anger that, when directed constructively, addresses injustice but, when uncontrolled, leads to harm and resentment.

Description:
Managed properly, wrath becomes assertiveness, advocating for positive change while respecting others. For instance, standing up against unfair treatment can bring about improvement. However, uncontrolled wrath leads to resentment, harm, and isolation and damaging relationships.

Threshold:
Pride in righteousness represents the tipping point for wrath. When anger becomes a justification for causing harm, it detaches from compassion and becomes self-serving. This pride leads to resentment, retaliation, and conflict, tearing down rather than building up.

Patience

Definition:
The ability to endure difficulty or delays with calmness, promoting thoughtful responses and empathy.

Description:
Patience tempers anger, encouraging thoughtful actions and compassion. Moderate consumption supports meaningful relationships and understanding. For example, listening carefully during a disagreement can lead to a better resolution. Yet, too much patience can lead to passivity, making it challenging to assert your needs or set boundaries.

Threshold:
Passivity marks the tipping point for patience. When patience masks fear of confrontation, it allows harmful behaviours and ignores your needs. This passivity leads to silence in the face of injustice, creating resentment and unmet needs.

Envy

Definition:
A desire for what others have, which can motivate growth or, if excessive, breed resentment and dissatisfaction.

Description:
When balanced, envy acts as a catalyst for self-reflection and personal improvement. For instance, admiring a colleague's success might inspire you to develop your skills. However, unchecked envy leads to constant comparison, diminishing gratitude and undermining self-worth.

Threshold:
Comparison marks the tipping point for envy. When envy turns into measuring your worth against others, it erodes self-esteem and fuels resentment. This comparison breeds bitterness, undermining self-worth, and prevents self-acceptance.

Kindness

Definition:
A compassionate approach to others, involving goodwill and support, tempered by self-respect to prevent self-neglect.

Description:
Kindness transforms envy by promoting appreciation for others' success. Balanced kindness supports others while maintaining your needs. For example, celebrating a friend's achievement without feeling diminished strengthens relationships. In excess, though, kindness may lead to self-neglect, prioritising others' needs over your well-being.

Threshold:
Over-accommodation marks the tipping point for kindness. When kindness seeks validation through others, it leads to self-sacrifice and weakened boundaries. This over-accommodation results in self-neglect and prevents healthy, balanced relationships.

Pride

Definition:
A healthy sense of self-worth and achievement, which can boost confidence but becomes harmful if it leads to arrogance.

Description:
When balanced, pride supports self-esteem and celebrates personal achievements without feeling superior. For instance, taking satisfaction in a job well done boosts confidence. Yet, when excessive, pride creates arrogance, weakening connections with others.

Threshold:
Pride tips over into entitlement. When pride slips into believing you're superior, it severs the connection to humility and empathy. This entitlement fuels arrogance and isolation, damaging relationships and stifling growth.

Humility

Definition:
An awareness of your limitations, promoting openness to growth and valuing others without undermining yourself.

Description:
Humility tempers pride by promoting self-awareness and respect for others. Practised moderately, it values others' worth without diminishing yours. For example, acknowledging a team member's contribution while recognising your role enhances collaboration. However, too much humility can lead to self-doubt, excessive deference, and undervaluing your abilities.

Threshold:
Self-doubt marks the tipping point for humility. When humility becomes insecure, it leads to excessive submission and a lack of self-worth. This self-doubt invites exploitation and prevents authentic self-expression.

3.3
Shame, Blame, and Guilt

The Path to Growth: Constructive Uses of Shame, Blame, and Guilt

Shame, blame, and guilt are often considered negative. But when used constructively, they can promote growth and accountability in the LCS. This chapter examines these powerful emotions, along with others, to provide a balanced assessment. After examining several instances, it becomes clear that both the positive and negative aspects of concepts like shame contribute to genuine self-discovery and progress in the virtual realm. This viewpoint promotes introspection, helping you tap into the potential of your emotions as a driving force, not an obstacle.

This section acts as a lookup table for exploring key emotional concepts, their roles, and their limitations. Each entry provides a clear definition, explains how the emotion can be constructive, and highlights its tipping point—the threshold where its value turns into harm. By understanding these emotional dynamics, you can recognise when emotions support growth and when they become obstacles. This awareness empowers you to engage consciously with feelings like shame, blame, guilt, and resentment, transforming them into tools for self-reflection and progress rather than sources of stagnation or harm.

Title:
The concept's title provides a clear identifier.

Definition:
A concise explanation of the concept's essential features and importance.

Description:
A detailed examination of the concept, including its functions, impacts, and practical applications, with examples.

Threshold:
The point where the concept stops being beneficial or manageable and becomes harmful or overwhelming. This highlights its limitations and potential risks.

Shame

Definition:
Feeling regret or discomfort about your actions or qualities, promoting self-reflection and responsibility.

Description:
Shame can serve as a useful brake on impulsive behaviour, prompting you to think about your actions and take responsibility. In its healthy form, shame is brief and leads to constructive self-assessment without harming your self-esteem. For example, if you say something hurtful to a friend, feeling ashamed might motivate you to apologise and consider how to communicate better. However, excessive shame can turn into self-loathing and deep insecurity, trapping you fearing judgement and preventing growth.

Threshold:
The tipping point for shame is self-criticism. When self-reflection turns into harsh self-criticism, shame becomes an endless cycle of negative judgement. This self-criticism fuels insecurity and stops you from moving forward.

Blame

Definition:
Assigning responsibility for a fault or mistake, used to clarify accountability constructively.

Description:
Blame, when used appropriately, can help clarify who is responsible and address misunderstandings or errors. Practised fairly, it is limited to the situation and encourages learning without causing resentment or defensiveness. For example, if a project at work fails because someone missed a deadline, acknowledging their role can help the team improve processes. However, excessive blame becomes divisive, leading to defensiveness and preventing self-reflection. This imbalance can weaken relationships and hinder personal growth.

Threshold:
The tipping point for blame is deflection. When accountability becomes a way to avoid your responsibility, blame turns into a tool for division, creating resentment and defensiveness instead of understanding and growth.

Guilt

Definition:
Feeling responsible or remorseful for a wrongdoing, often prompting empathy and a desire to make amends.

Description:
Guilt can inspire empathy and motivate you to make things right, supporting moral growth and self-awareness. Healthy guilt is temporary and focussed on specific actions, leading to positive changes without lingering regret. For instance, if you forget a friend's birthday, feeling guilty might prompt you to apologise and plan a belated celebration. However, excessive guilt becomes chronic, trapping you in cycles of self-punishment and preventing you from moving forward.

Threshold:
The tipping point for guilt is self-punishment. When guilt becomes self-directed blame, it turns into an ongoing need for atonement. This self-punishment keeps you stuck in regret, blocking growth and forgiveness.

Regret

Definition:
Feeling sorrow or disappointment over a past action or missed opportunity, which can guide self-awareness and encourage future growth.

Description:
Regret, when constructive, helps you recognise mistakes and make positive adjustments. In moderation, it highlights areas for improvement without dwelling excessively on the past. For example, if you regret not taking a job offer, you might be more proactive with future opportunities. However, when regret becomes chronic, it promotes self-blame and a sense of loss, anchoring you in past mistakes and limiting your ability to move forward.

Threshold:
The tipping point for regret is rumination. When regret fixates on the past rather than guiding improvement, it becomes a loop of self-criticism. This rumination traps you in over-analysis, preventing you from embracing new opportunities and learning from experiences.

Jealousy

Definition:
Feeling insecure or envious over something someone else has, often stemming from fear of loss or inadequacy.

Description:
Jealousy can highlight areas where your needs or desires feel unmet, guiding you to reflect on your aspirations. In a balanced form, it serves as an opportunity for self-reflection, helping you recognise and address your personal goals. For instance, feeling jealous of a friend's promotion might motivate you to pursue career development. However, unchecked jealousy turns into resentment and mistrust, straining relationships and breeding insecurity.

Threshold:
The tipping point for jealousy is comparison. When jealousy leads to constant comparison, it replaces self-awareness with insecurity, allowing resentment to grow and eroding trust in yourself and others.

Resentment

Definition:
A deep feeling of bitterness or anger towards someone you believe has wronged you.

Description:
Resentment can alert you to unresolved issues or injustices, motivating you to set boundaries or resolve conflicts. In its healthy form, it encourages self-assertion and protects against mistreatment. For example, feeling resentful about a colleague taking credit for your work might prompt you to address the issue assertively. However, when prolonged, resentment becomes self-destructive, creating emotional walls and leading to chronic bitterness that poisons relationships and prevents healing.

Threshold:
The tipping point for resentment is rumination. When resentment festers, it keeps you locked in cycles of anger and blame, turning past hurts into barriers to personal growth and positive relationships.

Empathy

Definition:
The ability to understand and share the feelings of another, promoting connection and compassion.

Description:
Empathy strengthens relationships by encouraging understanding and supportive responses, allowing you to connect deeply with others. Balanced empathy lets you be present for others without losing sight of your boundaries and well-being. For instance, comforting a friend distressed while also taking care of your emotional health maintains a healthy balance. However, excessive empathy can lead to emotional exhaustion and self-neglect, as you may have become overwhelmed by others' needs and emotions.

Threshold:
The tipping point for empathy is over-identification. When empathy crosses into over-identifying with others, it blurs the line between you and others, causing emotional fatigue and making it difficult to maintain healthy boundaries.

Balancing Authentic growth

Personal accountability, relationships, and self-growth can be influenced by various emotions, including shame, blame, guilt, regret, jealousy, resentment, and empathy. Balanced approaches to these emotions promote self-assessment, impulse control, and confidence. Blame can promote accountability and constructive responses, but excessive blame leads to defensiveness and strained relationships. Guilt can cultivate empathy and inspire restitution, but when it becomes self-punishment, it hampers growth and forgiveness. Regret can identify opportunities for improvement, but dwelling on the past prevents progress.

Jealousy can highlight unfulfilled desires, prompting self-reflection. However, excessive jealousy breeds insecurity and animosity, eroding trust. Resentment indicates unresolved issues or boundaries. If not addressed, it leads to bitterness, preventing healing. Empathy promotes understanding and compassion, nurturing meaningful relationships. However, excessive empathy can blur boundaries, leading to emotional exhaustion. Moderation, self-awareness, and setting boundaries are crucial for building a solid foundation for personal growth and positive relationships.

Balancing traits such as lust and chastity, gluttony and temperance, greed and charity, sloth and diligence nurtures personal growth, meaningful relationships, and self-discipline. These opposing forces, when balanced, promote moderation, self-respect, and purposeful action. Emotions like shame, guilt, jealousy, and empathy affect self-awareness and accountability, nurturing healthy relationships when managed properly.

Your constructive anger and pride support your resilience and progress. Meanwhile, patience, kindness, and humility encourage empathy and mutual respect. However, excess of these emotions can lead to impulsivity, self-criticism, or burnout. Therefore, maintaining a balance between these qualities is crucial for building fulfilling relationships and achieving personal growth.

Developing a balance of traits and emotions creates a strong foundation for personal growth, self-awareness, and positive relationships. But true growth requires understanding the impact of daily decisions on character development. Every choice, whether conscious or unconscious, impacts your journey towards progress, stagnation, or regression.

In the next chapter, "The Human Experience," you will explore a deeper framework of decision-making. You will consider how your actions guide you towards empathy, integrity, and connection. This builds on the balance of traits and emotions by examining how your choices influence your personal journey and your relationships with others.

4
The Human Experience

Building a life rooted in awareness and authenticity.

I grew up in a middle-class family with three brothers, living in a middle-class house in a middle-class village. While it was typical, there was drama, such as a stutter and being tall and slim, making me an easy target. After 30 years, I learned to overcome challenges, recognising their benefits. However, my earlier coping strategies became outdated and ineffective. Despite this, I had enough friends and was very curious about how things worked.

These experiences helped me develop strategies to reach the place I thought I wanted to be. The key word here is "thought" because I had one underlying strategy: I tried to fit in so that I would stop being a target. It felt like I was trying to make myself less noticeable, but I'm naturally tall, so it's hard for me to blend in. One strategy was to avoid excelling to avoid attention. At the same time, I had an insatiable appetite for data, information, and knowledge, which, I hoped, would eventually become wisdom, allowing me to lead a quiet, inner life.

This apparent contradiction between not wanting to excel and a hunger for knowledge led to frustration, strange behaviour and even nonsensical actions. I was aware of causing unhappiness in others. I tried to change my behaviour, but I didn't realise until about 15 years ago, that underlying and outdated strategies and programmes influenced me. My mind and willpower were more about fixing behaviours than solving problems.

Recently, an astrologer explained to me what had been happening to me during those contradictory years. He said, "I have been driving with my brakes on". The strategies and programmes were the brakes, while my desire to learn, discover, and create drove me towards a destination.

In "Navigating Human Experience," I examine how our reactions and choices shape our lives and influence our spiritual journeys. The following chapters—Habitual Reactions and Conscious Choices, Influencing Choices, and Life Paths—provide insights into the complex dynamics of human behaviour and decision-making.

The chapter on Habitual Reactions and Conscious Choices discusses the unconscious behaviours we exhibit in everyday life. These actions reflect our personal development, highlighting positive or negative patterns that impact our progress. Recognising these ingrained responses leads to increased self-awareness, nurturing authentic relationships based on empathy and mutual understanding. I examine the role of conscious decision-making in shaping our personal development. Every choice we make, big or small, affects our trajectory, either positively, negatively, or not at all. This chapter emphasises the value of self-reflection and deliberate decision-making.

The chapter "Choices Influenced" explores how both personal and external factors shape our decisions, highlighting the importance of self-reflection in shaping our character and creating opportunities for growth.

The Life Paths chapter describes three types of journeys: genuine growth, shortcuts, and corruption. Our decisions determine which path we take, influencing our spiritual development. This chapter examines the relationship between emotions, external factors, and the pursuit of true growth, emphasising the importance of facing challenges.

These chapters collectively offer a framework for understanding how habitual reactions, conscious choices, and the paths we take influence our human experience. Reflecting on these themes can deepen our awareness of ourselves and our connections to the larger Consciousness guiding our journey.

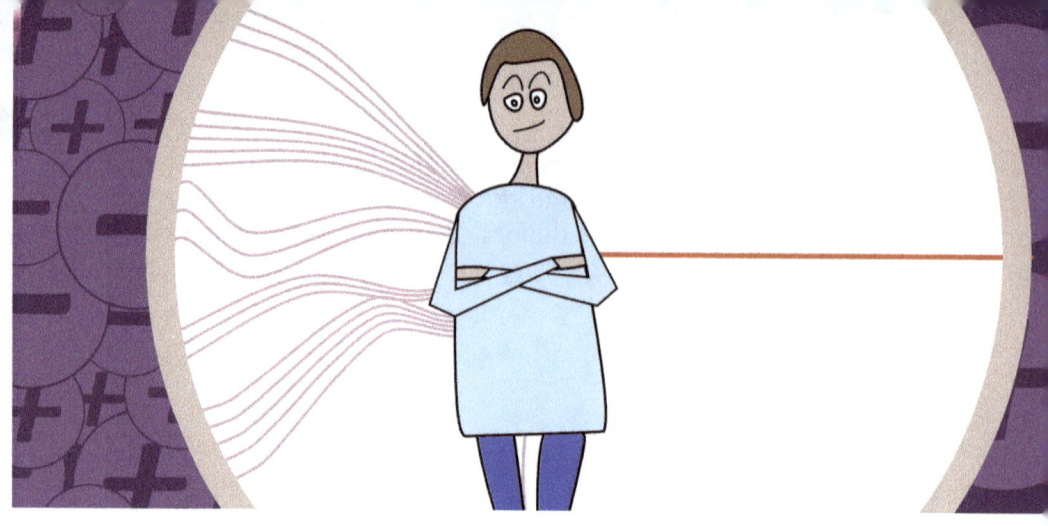

4.1
Habitual Reactions and Conscious Choices

Where Habit Meets Intention: A Journey of Growth

Your reactions to daily situations reveal much about your growth. Habitual reactions indicate where you stand on the spectrum between love and fear, and low and high entropy. These default reactions reflect your tendencies and behaviours, showing you who you truly are. By becoming aware of them, you can choose to engage more consciously and return to the path of genuine growth. Each response, especially towards others, is a chance to enhance your empathy and understanding.

In this exploration, you will examine how these automatic responses reflect your current growth. I will look at the consequences of default reactions, how they reinforce negative patterns, and their impact on relationships. In this chapter I also discuss the cycle of fear, the need for awareness, the importance of re-evaluating your choices, the potential for regret, and the necessity of active engagement.

Understanding the distinction between habitual reactions and conscious responses is crucial. While it can be tempting to respond based on social norms, learned behaviours can mask your true emotions, preventing authentic engagement with yourself and others.

As you explore these reactions, you will highlight how they influence your personal growth journey. Recognising the interaction between your innate responses and learned behaviours allows you to engage more meaningfully in your development.

Next, you will explore the consequences of these automatic responses, examining how they can reinforce negative patterns and affect your relationships. By understanding these dynamics, you can cultivate a more intentional approach to your interactions, leading to a more meaningful connection with yourself and Consciousness.

Habitual Reaction Framework

Default Reactions and Growth
Your default reactions in daily life often reflect your level of personal growth. When you respond automatically—ignoring what others say or dismissing their needs—you halt your potential for empathy and deeper connection. These habitual responses become like outdated routines, repeating without thought. To grow, you need to periodically reassess these patterns, allowing yourself to remain open to change and encouraging flexibility in your responses.

Negative Patterns and Their Effects
Not examined habits can reinforce negative patterns, impacting your relationships and limiting personal growth. When you respond out of habit rather than intention, you risk creating emotional distance and misunderstandings, which weaken your bonds with others. Negative patterns, left unchecked, harden over time, making change more challenging but also more essential.

Awareness and Intentional Choice
Being aware of your habitual reactions is the first step towards intentional growth. Awareness enables you to notice patterns that may hold you back, and this recognition is vital for making conscious choices. Each automatic response is an opportunity to pause and consider a more mindful approach, helping you align your behaviours with your personal growth goals.

Engagement for Transformation

Active engagement with others enriches your life and strengthens connections. By choosing to respond thoughtfully, you create meaningful interactions that encourage emotional growth, both for yourself and those around you.

Observing your negative reactions, even the patterns you'd rather avoid, gives you a chance to pause and reflect. Each moment of awareness—whether it shows you frustration, impatience, or avoidance—asks you: Is this who I am? Is this how I want to live and grow? Honest answers to these questions help clarify who you are now and that you hope to become.

As you explore your responses, you start to see each choice nudging you in a certain direction. Some choices build your compassion and integrity, others may feel like convenient shortcuts that steer you off course, and a few might even distance you from your truest self. By noticing these small shifts, you realise that every reaction, every choice, is shaping your path forward. This awareness can guide you towards a life of deeper purpose, integrity, and meaning.

Stepping back in the heat of the moment or reflecting on your mistakes later can be challenging and sometimes painful. Confronting these parts of yourself stirs discomfort, but it is essential for growth. In a later chapter on Authenticity, you'll explore how to safely become honest with yourself, addressing the root causes behind these reactions. This honest approach will help lessen your negative responses, making future reflections less painful and more empowering.

The Spectrum of Life's Choices

When you observe your reactions, especially those that challenge you, you begin to recognise how each choice shapes your character and guides you along your path in life. Even small decisions can either contribute to your growth or sometimes hold you back. Through honest self-reflection, you start to see where you might shift your responses, allowing you to approach life with greater purpose and integrity. This awareness helps you align your choices with whom you genuinely want to become.

Looking closely, you see that life isn't shaped by a single choice but by a broad spectrum of paths you continually encounter. Some of these paths lead to genuine growth, others offer tempting shortcuts, and a few may even draw you into decline. These are easy examples to recognise, but they are part of a much larger range of possibilities, with countless variations.

This framework provides a view of the different directions your Soul might take when facing life's challenges. Each choice—whether rooted in growth, convenience, or decline—guides your Soul's journey along a spectrum, moving it towards love and empathy or, alternatively, towards fear and disconnection.

At the positive end of the spectrum, your Soul may choose genuine growth, approaching life's challenges with openness and love. This path strengthens empathy, resilience, and a capacity to care for others. With each lifetime, experiences build naturally towards growth, as the simulation provides a fresh start by clearing memories, allowing new lessons to unfold.

Closer to the negative end lies the temptation to take shortcuts. Your Soul may pursue temporary gains or easy solutions by relying on external forces, gaining power or insight without the depth of personal growth. These choices lead to stagnation, as true progress requires self-effort rooted in love. The simulation does not reward or punish this path but allows its consequences to unfold, often creating cycles of stalled growth across lifetimes.

At the far negative end, a path of decline exists, marked by choices that lead to disconnection and degradation. Under the influence of destructive forces or harmful influences, your Soul may act in ways that harm yourself or others, reinforcing patterns of fear and isolation. Over time, such choices may erode your Soul's quality to the point that it no longer aligns with human experiences, leading to a lower form of existence in future lives.

This expansive, unbiased environment allows your Soul to explore its path, whether towards growth, stagnation, or decline. Through these choices, your Soul encounters the natural outcomes of its actions, gradually learning how each decision shapes its journey and its connections with others.

Choices in a Simulation Called Life

In this unbiased learning environment, all paths coexist without judgement. The simulation provides a space where your Soul:

> *Can pursue genuine growth, moving towards the low-entropy end of the spectrum through conscious effort.*
>
> *May choose shortcuts, drifting closer to the high-entropy end as it seeks escape or convenience by relying on external influences.*
>
> *Can also select harmful paths, experiencing a decline over lifetimes as it moves deeper into the negative end of the spectrum.*

The impartiality of this environment ensures there is no moral judgement—only natural consequences. Souls acting with love and empathy experience growth, while those choosing shortcuts may find themselves stalled, unable to progress. Souls that turn towards harmful actions face a gradual decline. This range of experiences is essential, as the purpose of this environment is to offer a full array of learning opportunities, allowing Souls to exercise their free will and encounter the natural outcomes of their choices.

In this way, Simulation Theory and its pathways fit within a broader cause-and-effect system. This Consciousness framework allows your Soul to experience the consequences of its actions, whether they lead to growth, stagnation, or decline. By recognising the importance of your habitual reactions and the decisions you make, you gain tools to navigate your journeys with greater clarity. This awareness deepens your understanding of yourself and reinforces your interconnectedness with others.

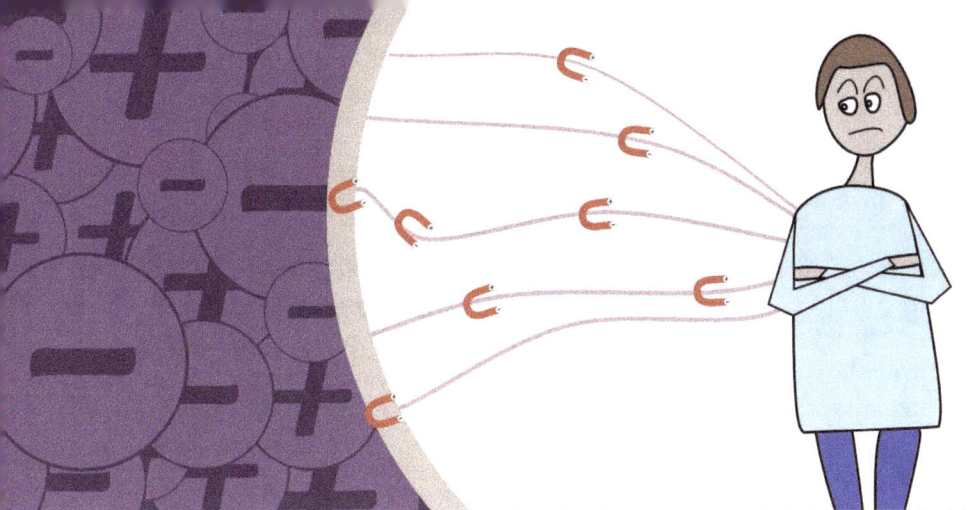

4.2

Choices Influenced

How Hidden Influences Guide Your Path and Soul's Growth

Consciousness provides an environment where Souls make decisions that shape their growth, stagnation, or decline. It does not impose outcomes; instead, it offers space for experiences. The quality of a Soul—measured by its ability to navigate situations with love and empathy—determines its position along a spectrum from good to evil, low entropy to high entropy, and love to fear.

The simulation is designed to facilitate experience rather than dictate outcomes. Consciousness allows Souls to learn and grow through their choices, leading to a wide variety of experiences. Unfortunately, part of this experience includes accidents and unexpected negative events. These events occur due to the free will of others, whether for good or ill. Consciousness has no favourites; it seeks experiences through the diverse actions of many Souls. Each Soul adds experiences to its data package and contributes to the collective understanding of Consciousness (the Larger Consciousness System). Negative experiences are part of life.

Some negative experiences can be devastating, making life challenging to cope with. However, most situations present challenges—planned, unplanned, expected, or unexpected—that force us to choose how to react. In these moments, our true character is revealed. When we respond to our deepest, purest emotions, the Soul speaks, and both the positive and negative aspects of our nature come to the surface.

It is admirable to react harmoniously and lovingly, but the less favourable aspects of our character—such as unkindness or selfishness—also deserve attention. Understanding these traits can provide valuable insights into areas for personal growth. Recognising negative reactions does not imply a preference for them over positive behaviours; instead, they serve as opportunities for self-reflection and development.

Life provides valuable opportunities for introspection. By observing our reactions, we identify areas where growth is possible and take steps to improve our responses. Recognising the potential for improvement is essential for personal development, and it is vital to actively engage in this process.

In life, we constantly confront choices. Some are obvious, while many are not because they have become habitual. These choices may not seem significant because they have become ingrained in our being. For instance, how we react to those closest to us often goes not examined. We may fail to truly listen to what a loved one is saying, feeling we've heard "this same story" too many times. As a result, we often give a default reaction, if any at all.

Influencing Choices
Life is a journey shaped by choices, each guiding us along unique paths of personal and spiritual growth. This text explores three paths—Genuine Growth, Shortcuts, and Corruption—that simplify how we navigate a cycle of emotions, intentions, thoughts, and actions. Each choice contributes to this cycle of cause and effect, moving us towards either love and harmony or fear and disharmony.

I named these paths Genuine Growth, Shortcuts, and Corruption, mainly to refer to them more easily. Each choice, whether large or small, directs this cycle towards creating a patchwork of 'good' and 'bad' qualities. These three example paths illustrate how circumstances, mindset, and other factors influence us to make certain choices. The paths act like caricatures, making subtleties more explicit and thus recognisable.

My central thesis is that many choices are a double-edged sword. Not only do we learn from 'bad' choices, 'good' choices can also steer us away from authentic growth. Anger can cloud our thinking, but it also brings clarity. When handled with care, anger cuts through apathy, pushing us to take careful and meaningful steps towards a better outcome. Spiritual practices like meditation unify intention and action, but their real value comes from balancing them with our involvement in the world around us, or they result in escapism.

NHI

A more controversial topic is introducing the idea of external and normally unseen presences. ST and the LCS fully support the concept of many kinds of Consciousness (individuated units of Consciousness in Tom's language). The main reason for writing this book is that somehow the impression is created, or the perception emerges, that Non-Human Intelligences (NHI) surround us but do not significantly influence us.

Non-Human Intelligences (NHI):

Non-Human Intelligences (NHIs) are conscious, intelligent entities that exist both within and beyond human perception. They operate within a framework that aligns with Simulation Theory and the LCS. Some NHIs may have a physical form, while others engage through dreams, symbols, or altered states. They connect selectively with individuals, sometimes targeting vulnerable people or responding to openness, forming long-term associations that follow motives outside human concepts of morality.

NHIs actively alter both perception and physical reality, using advanced technology or inherent abilities compatible with the simulation model. Their actions are partly comprehensible but still mysterious. Though some act alone, many likely belong to a larger, coordinated civilisation, which may influence or direct their interactions with humans. Their involvement ranges from subtle cultural shifts to significant individual impacts, including influencing memory, perception, and physical events. The aims of NHIs vary but may include gathering information, experimentation, or influencing human progress, although their intentions are purely pragmatic and differ from human ethics.

These NHIs typically go undetected by the five human senses, and laboratory instruments are ill-equipped to provide a conclusive picture of what we are dealing with. Consequently, the concept of NHI is conveniently pushed into categories like 'coincidences,' 'hallucinations,' 'vivid imagination,' or old conspiracy theories. At the same time, countless reports, both anecdotal and observed by credible third parties, tell a very different story.

Throughout history, both anecdotal accounts and documented cases suggest that NHIs' influences are present yet difficult for modern science to measure or verify. Such phenomena are mostly dismissed as hallucinations or products of an overactive imagination, sidelined by rational discourse. However, these incidents bear striking similarities to stories of individuals who, through intense spiritual practices, encounter unexplainable experiences. The boundary between the real and the imagined, the tangible and the intangible, blurs when people enter states where normal laws of perception and physical matter no longer apply.

Unseen forces within the LCS can, under certain unique conditions, manifest directly into physical reality. These manifestations challenge the foundations of contemporary physics, contradicting established principles such as Newton's laws of motion, which govern the predictable behaviour of objects. Such occurrences suggest that influences beyond the scope of known physics—forces that operate outside conventional frameworks of cause and effect—push the boundaries of our understanding of the material world.

Whether prompted by an external influence or emerging through a disciplined pursuit of transcendence, history presents instances of phenomena that disrupt accepted definitions of reality. These extraordinary events, though rare, raise important questions about the true nature of Consciousness and its ability to interact with and alter physical reality.

Fra Giuseppe da Copertino
One well-documented example is the volo estatico, or elevation in ecstasy, of Fra Giuseppe da Copertino, who was posthumously canonised by Pope Clement XIII on 16 July 1767 as Sanctus Josephus a Cupertino. During those times, opinions, and reactions varied strongly regarding the expression and nature of so-called supernatural phenomena. Regardless of how opinions and reactions to unexplainable events and experiences have developed over the course of human evolution, they continue to occur.

The terms "supernatural" and "unexplainable" are in quotation marks because their meanings vary significantly depending on the context. Outside the LCS and spiritual practices, "supernatural" usually suggests something beyond natural laws or logic. However, within LCS and spiritual practices, these ideas are not considered mysterious or beyond comprehension. Instead, they are regarded as a logical and natural part of reality.

In the rest of this chapter, I discuss topics that may provoke strong reactions in some readers. Many communities develop firm ideas about what is right and wrong, which can turn into fixed beliefs or dogmas. This has both positive and negative effects. For individuals, such beliefs can support personal growth but may also limit it. Within groups, many beliefs become rigid and closed to new perspectives. Please keep in mind that I present these ideas as points on a spectrum, highlighting the extremes for clarity, though most human behaviour falls somewhere in the middle.

Over-referencing

Meditation reveals that reality can be shaped by our intentions, emotions, and habits. However, while it deepens self-awareness, over-relying on it may make it an escape from daily life. Practised in balance, meditation serves as a tool for growth rather than an end in itself. When grounded in daily life, meditation supports self-awareness, helping us engage with the world rather than escape from it. This grounded approach to growth also involves meeting challenges with compassion, as seen when we listen patiently rather than reacting impulsively. Authentic growth is reflected in our responses to challenges; it's about cultivating compassion and resilience, like choosing to listen with patience instead of reacting impulsively.

The difference between true realisation and "over-referencing" is crucial. "Over-referencing" refers to an over-reliance on external insights, such as meditative or mystical experiences, to the point that they start guiding one's thoughts and actions more than practical reasoning. A key distinction here is between over-referencing and true intuition. While over-referencing can disconnect us from grounded reasoning, intuition emerges naturally when we are attuned to our true Self.

A danger that lurks around the spiritual corner is that one identifies with experiences that happen in another realm. These experiences and the Self that experiences it can become part of a new persona, or mask. In effect, this new dreamlike character could begin to influence choices in "Life on Earth". But these different realities have different growth opportunities and need different logic to function. Intuition can be considered the Soul's natural way of communicating with our conscious awareness, through signals we feel physically or thoughts that arise spontaneously. When meditation becomes a regular part of life, the mind and body are naturally more receptive to these subtle messages. This is the healthy path: staying connected to your inner Self while fully engaging in the world around you.

When we are in tune with our authentic Self—for example, achieved through a default meditative state—communication naturally occurs beyond our conscious awareness. This communication connects us with our Soul, other Souls, and the LCS itself. Rather than requiring deliberate thought, this exchange is guided by our intentions, desires, and emotions within the broader realm of Consciousness.

Default Meditative State
This is a natural, effortless state of calm awareness. It allows a steady, neutral focus on whatever task is at hand without any need to control thoughts or apply techniques. It isn't something you consciously enter; it simply arises naturally. The purpose is to maintain mental clarity and ease tension, rather than to gain deep self-awareness or spiritual insight. This state quietly stays in the background, keeping you grounded and balanced as you go through the day.

As we begin exploring meditation, distinguishing between messages from our imagination, our true Self, other Souls, or the LCS can be challenging. Insights come and go, feeling unclear or fleeting. With practice, we develop a deeper self-awareness that helps us recognise which messages truly come from within and which stem from external sources. This discernment is essential, as not all guidance aligns with our highest path or intentions.

However, when driven by emotions like fear or anger, this communication can attract non-incarnate entities whose intentions may diverge from our growth—or may even work against it.

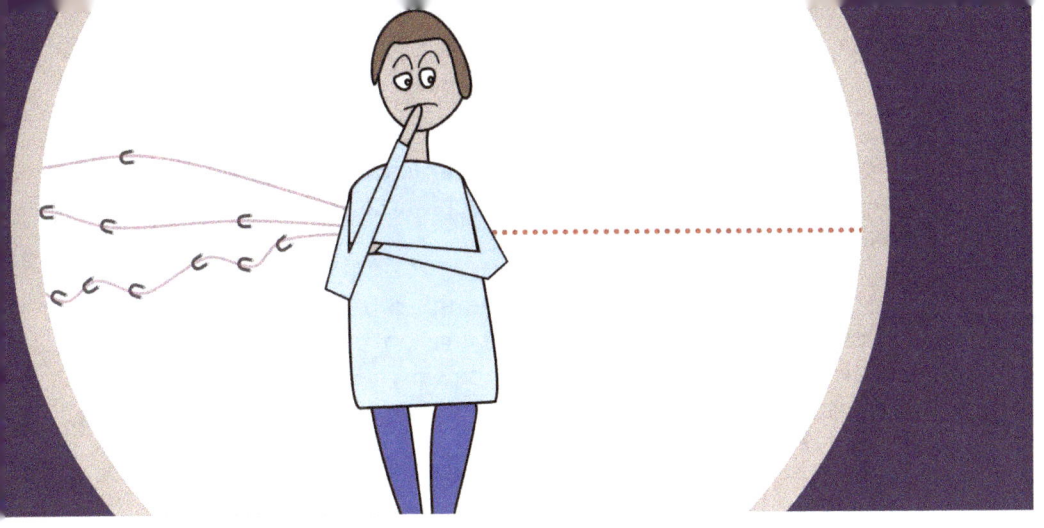

4.3
Life Paths

From Habit to Intention: Taking Responsibility for Growth

The human experience is a journey of growth (or decline) and self-discovery, shaped by our choices, reactions, and the paths we take. Through facing challenges, reflecting on our actions, and reevaluating our strategies, we uncover deeper truths about ourselves and our connection to the world. This chapter explores how habitual reactions, conscious choices, and life paths define not only individual growth but also our broader spiritual journey.

I draw on both personal experiences and broader insights. The following sections examine three unconscious patterns that drive daily responses, the factors that influence decisions, and the consequences of the paths we choose. Whether we seek genuine growth, fall into shortcuts, or risk corruption, each choice contributes to the trajectory of our development. Reflecting on these dynamics equips us with the tools to navigate life with greater purpose, clarity, and alignment with our authentic selves.

I invite you to examine your reactions and decisions, offering a framework to recognise and transform outdated patterns. This chapter emphasises the importance of intentional engagement and self-awareness in shaping a life of meaning and connection, both within yourself and with the larger Consciousness System that guides us all.

In this section, I explore the complexity of personal growth. I present three distinct paths you might recognise on your journey towards self-improvement. We begin with the "Genuine Growth Path", a route that embraces gradual, internal development, emphasising self-compassion, patience, and the acceptance of both progress and setbacks.

In contrast, I analyse the "Shortcut Path", a tempting alternative that promises rapid results through reliance on external forces, such as Non-Human Intelligences (NHIs), one's own Soul, or even the Level of Consciousness (LCS). While seemingly efficient, this path may bypass the crucial inner work necessary for lasting transformation.

Finally, I navigate the treacherous terrain of the "Corruption Path", where unresolved trauma, and a resulting inner void, can make individuals vulnerable to external influences, leading to dependency and a detachment from the authentic self. By understanding these diverse approaches, we gain valuable insights into the complexities of personal growth and the importance of choosing a path that nurtures genuine, enduring change.

Genuine Growth Path

This approach to personal growth accepts both gradual and sudden progress, viewing emotions like anger or frustration as signs of development rather than setbacks. It encourages a focus on progress over perfection, with self-compassion and patience as essential qualities. Growth is seen in more measured responses to challenges and a more profound understanding of oneself, regardless of how fast it happens.

Authentic growth comes from meeting life's challenges with love, empathy, and understanding. Rather than seeking external rewards, this path promotes kindness and connection, allowing compassion to return naturally through our interactions with others. As we embrace this process, the Soul gradually expands its capacity for love and harmony, evolving toward a richer sense of fulfilment.

True growth means acting with compassion rather than fear or self-interest. While meditation and spiritual practices support this journey, they can't replace the real-world experiences that drive genuine transformation. Engaging fully with life's challenges is what promotes lasting growth.

Instead of direct intervention, Consciousness may guide us subtly through synchronistic events—meaningful coincidences that encourage growth. For instance, missing a train and meeting someone important to our journey on the next one is one way these moments can unfold. Such events suggest that life, though seemingly indifferent, could present growth opportunities when we remain open to them.

Each interaction and choice offer us a chance to move closer to love and kindness—or further away. Growth is rarely consistent; we might advance in some areas while struggling in others. At the end of each lifetime, this balance is reviewed at the level of Consciousness (LCS). Like the idea of St. Peter at the gate—but without judgement—this review highlights what went well and where growth is still needed, preparing the Soul for its next journey.

In daily life, judgement is a practical tool for navigating choices. Rather than something negative, it helps us discern how our actions align with our values. By reflecting on our intentions and responses, we learn to make decisions that support kindness and understanding. This judgement doesn't involve blame or harsh reactions; instead, it offers an objective view of our progress, highlighting both strengths and areas for improvement. Rooted in intuition and careful evaluation, this form of judgement guides us to respond thoughtfully without acting on every judgement outwardly. It supports personal growth and helps lay a balanced foundation for the Soul's journey ahead.

A meditative state occurs when brain activity shifts into the theta frequency range, about 4 Hz to 8 Hz. This range, linked to relaxation, creativity, and introspection, enables the mind to enter a calm and receptive mode. Many activities—such as meditation, listening to music, connecting closely with others, or simply unwinding—can help reach this state, allowing the mind to disengage from active thought.

Meditation is one way to build focus and self-awareness, but it isn't the only path to growth. Joyful and mindful moments in daily life can have similar effects, deepening our sense of presence and mental flexibility. In the theta range, the mind quiets its analytical processes, opening to insights and a restorative calm that can be accessed through various everyday experiences.

While meditation and mindful activities enhance our focus and self-awareness, it's important to recognise that not all paths toward growth are created equal. Some approaches may yield quick results but lack the depth necessary for lasting change.

Shortcut Path

Growth is a natural and unpredictable process, full of ups and downs, so it's no wonder people might look for faster, easier ways to achieve it. One such approach involves interacting with Non-Human Intelligences (NHIs), one's Soul, or even the LCS. I call this the "Shortcut Path," as it aims to make growth quicker and less turbulent.

The Shortcut Path relies on external forces, like NHIs or even one's Soul, to achieve rapid results that can bypass the need for inner work. Methods such as magic or manifesting are examples, offering immediate outcomes but when overdone, at the expense of deeper and personal development. By seeking quick fixes, these approaches can overlook the essential lessons found in real-world challenges and social interactions.

When I talk about "deeper inner work," I mean a process focussed on building authenticity by addressing secrets, traumas, and fears. This involves confronting and integrating difficult aspects of oneself using approaches like therapy, mindfulness, or creative outlets, such as fictional writing based on personal experiences. My method suggests a progression: first, sharing secrets anonymously or with trusted friends; then moving to a private group; and finally, sharing openly with the public. I delve into this process more deeply in a later chapter.

While deeper inner work supports the journey to authenticity, my approach defines authenticity as a separate, specific path. This path aligns with the principles of inner work but isn't limited to them. Deeper inner work can include exploring unknown realms, such as using one's intention to affect reality. However, it's crucial to understand where the desire to alter reality stems from. Is it to avoid difficult physical tasks or challenging social interactions? Or is it a genuine curiosity and deliberate testing of how reality functions?

From Greed to Understanding

In one of my experiments, I used magic to influence lottery outcomes. After 32 focussed attempts, I experienced minor successes, like matching three or four numbers and winning small amounts. But once I accepted that "yes, this works" and recognised that I couldn't get beyond a certain level, these results disappeared entirely. It was as if the LCS wanted me to confirm the technique's validity yet also convey that this approach wasn't meant for sustained or deeper gain. This experience taught me that while shortcuts can produce temporary benefits, they ultimately offer limited growth potential.

Shortcuts rely on either external influence or deliberate interaction. With external influence, entities or unseen forces may subtly affect outcomes without the individual's full awareness. By contrast, intended interaction, like a ritual or heartfelt prayer, sends a focussed message—whether to the Soul, Self, the LCS, or another unseen presence—expressing serious intent. While these methods may produce short-term effects, they generally do not build the internal development essential for lasting stability and growth.

Over time, shortcuts can lead to dependency. People may become locked into repetitive patterns, performing rituals not out of genuine choice but from a need for control or fear of negative consequences if they stop. In extreme cases, they might feel compelled to perform certain prayers or meditations in rigid ways, believing harm will result if they deviate. This dependency disempowers, replacing authentic self-connection with a fear-driven reliance that ultimately blocks genuine growth.

The LCS itself remains indifferent to the use of shortcuts, neither punishing nor rewarding them. However, relying on shortcuts reduces growth, as they allow us to circumvent challenges rather than face them directly. True growth requires engaging with life's obstacles, as these experiences build resilience, self-awareness, and empathy. While each life offers a fresh start with a reset in memory, lasting development arises only from sincere choices rooted in love and a willingness to confront difficulties, rather than taking shortcuts.

Corruption Path

When a Soul endures significant trauma or deep emotional wounds, an internal void often forms, making the individual more vulnerable to external influences. This void is not just a metaphorical gap; it reflects unhealed aspects of the Self, leaving the individual susceptible to external forces that may operate outside conscious awareness. Across human experience, psychological and spiritual perspectives alike suggest that trauma disrupts the cohesion of the Self, opening pathways for influences that infiltrate the mind and shape behaviour.

To fill this void, individuals often turn to external sources of identity or meaning, such as ideologies, charismatic leaders, or collective entities known as Egregores. These influences offer a sense of belonging or purpose, which can quickly turn into dependency when inner stability is lacking. Egregores, as collective thought forms shaped by shared beliefs, can exert a powerful pull on those seeking significance outside themselves. This attachment may advance strong loyalty or belief systems, causing individuals to align with ideologies or movements to fill internal gaps. Over time, this dependency can override personal discernment, limiting the individual's authentic connection to their Self.

An Egregore begins as a collective thought form, created and sustained by the shared intentions of a group. Over time, it can take on a degree of autonomy, exerting influence not to support individual growth but to preserve its existence. Souls, particularly those carrying unresolved trauma, may be drawn to these entities, substituting true self-connection with dependence on collective identity. In extreme cases, the influence may stem from a conscious, independent entity with its motivations, which can further lead a Soul off its growth path.

Beyond ideological influences, subtler forces may affect thoughts and behaviours, operating outside the individual's conscious control. Some people report experiencing voices or compulsions that feel foreign or find themselves acting in uncharacteristic ways. These voices or impulses can sometimes display knowledge or influence beyond the individual's usual awareness or personality, defying simple psychological explanation. Such occurrences have been noted across various therapeutic and spiritual contexts, leading some to consider the possibility of external influence.

This phenomenon can resemble a form of possession where the individual's autonomy is partially compromised. Emotions, intentions, thoughts, and actions may seem directed by an external presence with its intentions. These presences can vary in nature; some may act neutrally or even helpfully, while others seem to deepen the individual's trauma by manipulating emotions like fear, guilt, or anger. Certain spiritual practices, like exorcisms, aim to address these attachments by severing the influence and restoring the person's autonomy, reconnecting them with their authentic Self.

A common thread among those affected is unresolved trauma, feelings of unworthiness, or internalised shame. These unhealed wounds make them vulnerable to external forces that exploit unresolved pain. By feeding on negative emotions, these influences can maintain control, creating cycles of dependency, isolation, and fear that draw the individual further from genuine healing.

This pattern shows how trauma-induced susceptibility can open a person to various influences, some beyond psychological explanations and possibly originating from external forces that seek to occupy this internal void. Recognising these influences as both psychological and external provides a more comprehensive framework for understanding how trauma can leave individuals vulnerable to ideologies, attachments, and entities that exploit this openness. Addressing these influences requires not only psychological healing but also a strengthened connection to the Self, building resilience to prevent external forces from filling the gaps left by unhealed wounds.

Trauma, especially from early abuse, neglect, or other deeply unsettling experiences, often leads individuals to develop survival-based coping mechanisms. These responses—such as detachment, hyper vigilance, or aggression—act as shields, helping them manage overwhelming emotions or circumstances. Although initially protective, these strategies can solidify over time, becoming default habits that shape interactions and perspectives. Rooted in survival, such coping mechanisms often limit opportunities for authentic connection and empathy, creating a hardened barrier between the person and their true Self.

As these survival-driven patterns deepen, the individual's focus increasingly shifts towards maintaining psychological defences instead of furthering growth. This constant need for self-protection can overshadow curiosity, openness, and empathy, causing the individual to retreat into guarded isolation. Such isolation restricts the capacity for healthy relationships and reinforces the void left by unresolved trauma, making the Soul more susceptible to external attachments, ideologies, and entities. Over time, survival-based behaviours may override the internal drive for growth and self-awareness, causing the person to lose sight of their original path and purpose.

As this void grows, it becomes fertile ground for influences that reinforce stagnation or harm. Some individuals may cling to ideologies or group identities that validate their survival strategies, while others might form attachments to unseen entities that intensify feelings of isolation, anger, or fear. These attachments—whether ideological or spiritual—often feed on the individual's pain and reinforce survival-driven behaviours, distancing them further from authentic growth. Instead of healing, they become trapped in cycles of dependency on external validation or forces, moving further from self-reliance and inner harmony.

Ultimately, the Corruption Path shows how a survival-oriented approach distances the Soul from its true Self. By placing self-protection above vulnerability and relying on external attachments rather than inner resilience, individuals on this path find it increasingly difficult to return to love, empathy, and genuine self-awareness. These influences feed on unresolved trauma, turning potential opportunities for healing into patterns of stagnation or decline. Only by facing and healing these deep-seated wounds can one begin to reclaim the path of authentic growth, moving away from external dependence and towards a more integrated, self-directed life.

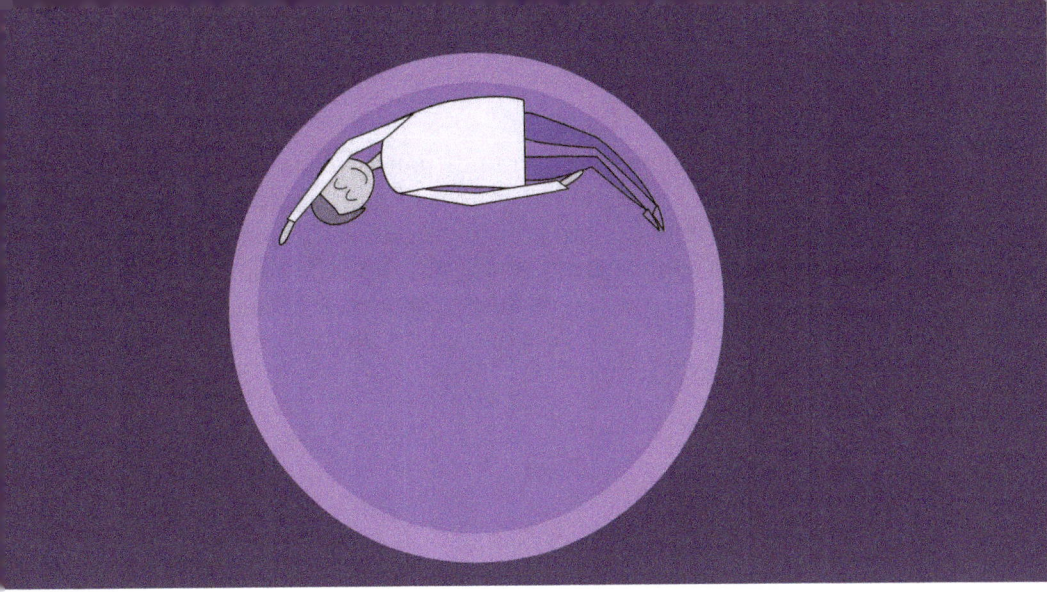

5
Echoes of the Infinite
Communicating with the Larger Consciousness System

*I*n the previous chapters, I explored what the LCS is and how it functions, emphasising the essential roles of the Soul and reincarnation in understanding who we are and what we can achieve. In the chapter on Forces, I examined various frameworks that influence our decisions—internal ones within our minds, external factors like society and culture, and less visible influences such as Non-Human Intelligence (NHI). In the chapter on Human Experiences, I focussed on the methods we use to navigate life, illustrating how our choices shift us between two fundamental poles: fear and love.

In this chapter, I aim to share practical methods for gaining greater influence over self-discovery and personal desires, showing how to channel these intentions through mental focus. I'll also discuss ways to interact with the LCS so that you can explore it firsthand using techniques like meditation or tools such as binaural beats. While I won't delve into the numerous worlds within the LCS—given that each person's experiences will differ—I'll focus on the logical aspects of the LCS that are relevant to this book. There are countless experiences in astral planes or other realms, but these explorations fall outside the scope of my narrative.

I wrote, in the chapter on reincarnation, about how Souls communicate across realms. Among other things, I used an analogy of a virtual reality game to explain how loved ones who have passed may subtly guide us, as if whispering gentle directions, such as a nudge to visit a meaningful place. In this chapter, I continue with communication, now focusing on communication from here to the LCS, and from the LCS to here.

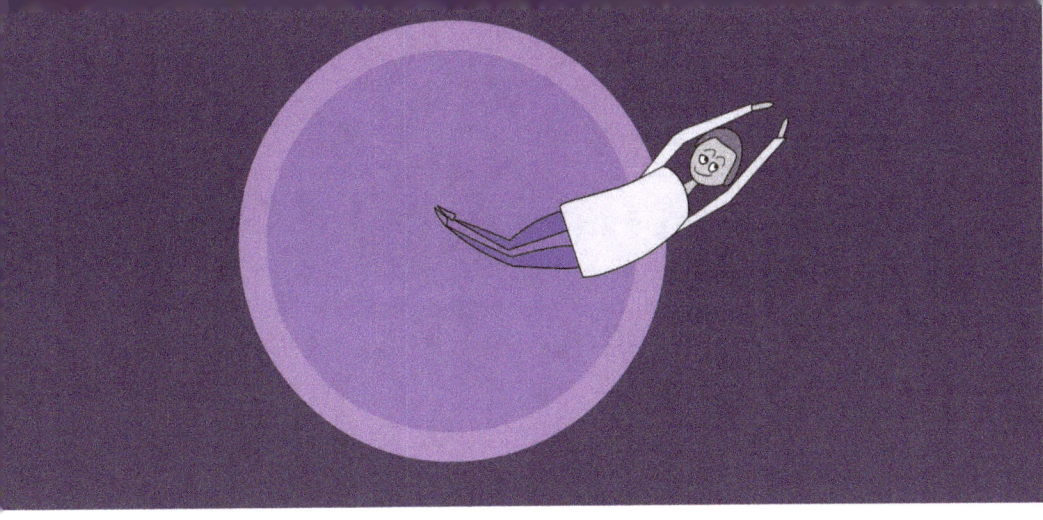

5.1
Passive and Active Interactions
Explorations in the LCS

You can connect and communicate with the LCS through various strategies, which I separate into primarily passive or active approaches. Each has unique advantages and challenges, and choosing the right one depends on your personal preferences and goals in engaging with the LCS. Here, I'll provide a high-level overview of these methods and share some examples, including meditation, binaural beats, remote viewing, affirmations, and manifesting.

In this section, I've organised various methods of how to interact with the LCS. To make this broad topic approachable and not overwhelming, I've broken down complex ideas into digestible parts. You'll find a balance of high-level overviews, straightforward explanations, and concise lists to help you grasp the essence of each approach without feeling overloaded.

You'll explore different methods—such as passive versus active techniques for interacting with the LCS—each followed by practical examples. The aim is to give you a roadmap, not a strict itinerary, giving you the freedom to explore what feels right for you at your pace.

Overall, this structure should feel more like a conversation than a course. Let yourself be curious, pause where you need, and know that each list, table, and example are here to simplify, not complicate, your journey.

Passive Methods

Getting in Touch with the LCS

In this approach, you let yourself be open and receptive to whatever comes from the LCS, without actively trying to connect. These techniques help you naturally tune in to the subtle energy of the LCS by relaxing your mind and letting impressions come on their own. You don't try to "make" anything happen; instead, you simply allow yourself to receive.

Examples of techniques: taking a shower, meditation, binaural beats, floating in water or float tanks, listening to white or pink noise, mindful breathing without goal, monotonous car driving, sitting on the train, premonitions

Pros

Ease of Practice:
You can integrate this approach seamlessly into your daily routines with minimal effort.

Reduced Resistance:
With less pressure to achieve specific outcomes, you'll find it easier to relax and connect authentically.

Enhanced Intuition:
As you stay open and receptive, you'll encourage your innate intuitive abilities to develop.

Cons

Unpredictable Results:
Without intentional focus, your experiences may vary or feel inconsistent.

Slower Progress:
Building a strong relationship with the LCS may take more time when you engage passively.

Potential for Distraction:
It's easy to get distracted by your surroundings or thoughts, which can disrupt the passive state and impact connection quality.

Exploring the LCS

With passive exploration, you let insights and impressions from the LCS come naturally, often as a byproduct of everyday activities. You might be doing something else, like daydreaming or journalling, when information from the LCS appears. It's less about directly asking for answers and more about observing what comes to you naturally.

Examples of techniques: journalling, daydreaming, intentional dreaming, keeping a coincidence or synchronicity journal, casual observation of people or places, unscripted visualisation or daydreaming, cloud watching or stargazing, and reading symbolic books or poetry

Pros:

Natural Flow:
You align with the LCS's inherent rhythms, creating a more harmonious exploration.

Depth of Understanding:
This method allows you to process and integrate LCS insights on a deeper, unaware (subconscious) level.

Flexibility:
You can adapt this approach to different states of Consciousness and schedules.

Cons:

Lack of Structure:
Without a clear method, you may find it challenging to navigate your explorations effectively.

Limited Control:
Relying on spontaneous experiences can make it challenging to reach specific exploration goals.

Potential Overwhelm:
With an abundance of subtle information, it's easy to feel overwhelmed without active focus.

Active Methods

Getting in Touch with the LCS

With active methods, you intentionally set out to connect with the LCS. These techniques involve putting focussed energy into the connection, setting specific intentions, and using practices that create a direct and conscious link. Here, you're more goal-oriented, clearly seeking a response or interaction from the LCS.

Examples of techniques: affirmations and manifesting, guided visualisation, chanting or mantra recitation, personal intention setting rituals, energy work, active listening to sacred music, expressive writing with intent

Pros

> *Clear Intentions:*
> You'll experience more consistent, measurable connections by setting defined goals and focussing your efforts.
>
> *Enhanced Control:*
> This approach gives you more influence over the nature and frequency of your interactions with the LCS.
>
> *Accelerated Engagement*
> By engaging actively, you'll likely build a meaningful relationship with the LCS more quickly.

Cons

> *Potential Strain:*
> Intense focus and effort can lead to mental fatigue or frustration if results take time to appear.
>
> *Risk of Imbalance:*
> Overemphasis on active methods can sometimes disrupt the natural flow of the connection.
>
> *Dependence on Techniques:*
> Relying heavily on specific practices may limit your adaptability in how you naturally could interact with the LCS.

Exploring the LCS

Active exploration means deliberately seeking experiences or information from the LCS with a clear purpose in mind. This approach involves structured techniques that guide you to go deeper into the connection. Through these methods, you might set specific questions, use symbolic tools, or enter focussed meditation to explore particular aspects of the LCS.

Examples of techniques: remote viewing, interactive meditation sessions, lucid dream exploration with set intentions, sensory deprivation, Kozyrev mirror, out-of-body experience (OBE) practices, symbolic, or divination tools (e.g., Tarot, Runes), intentional past life or Akashic Records exploration, focussed question meditation note: these are not recommendations and some techniques might open connections with others, like NHIs

Pros:

> *Directed Exploration:*
> With clear objectives and a structured approach, you'll be able to uncover targeted insights.
>
> *Enhanced Engagement:*
> Active participation lets you build a stronger, more dynamic relationship with the LCS.
>
> *Measurable Progress:*
> Structured methods help you track and assess the depth and quality of your interactions.

Cons

> *Resource Intensive:*
> To engage effectively, you'll need to invest time, effort, and sometimes specific tools or environments.
>
> *Risk of Overwhelm:*
> Intensive exploration can sometimes lead to information overload or emotional strain.
>
> *Possible Rigidity:*
> If you stick too strictly to certain techniques, you might limit the natural evolution of your connection with the LCS.
>
> *Possible negative mental effects:*
> You enter a vast domain with many unknowns; not everything has the best of interest at heart for you. You carry your fears and doubts with you into this vast environment, which influences your perception of your experiences, and your reaction to those experiences.

5.2

The Mechanics

A Passive and Active Approach

I aim to bring structure to my thinking. While I'm not claiming to always succeed, it's a goal, I actively work towards. As I reflect on my progress in experimenting with the LCS, I compiled a list of what I consider the core elements that influence change in this reality. Dean Radin, in his book Real Magic, discusses the fundamental elements of magic(k):

Divination:
Seeking knowledge of hidden or future events through various methods like tarot, astrology, or the I Ching.

Force of Will (Manifestation):
The focussed intention to influence reality through one's thoughts and beliefs. This is sometimes related to practices like intention setting, rituals, or visualisation aimed at producing real-world changes.

Theurgy (Evocation/Invocation):
Engaging with entities, such as spirits, deities, or archetypes, to access guidance, wisdom, or aid. This involves rituals and invocations to connect with these entities for personal or spiritual insight.

I find this list deeply inspiring, but to stay true to myself, I felt compelled to rework it and add a personal touch. My version emphasises encouraging goodness and love, though I recognise that individuals may use these same mechanics in different ways. While the items I list don't strongly focus on theurgical elements, such aspects can be incorporated if desired. Additionally, I have divided the list into active and passive parts: the active section pertains to actions you do, whereas the passive section relates to who you are.

Active

Attention:
Deepen focus and commitment through practices like meditation, which reinforce your goals. Singing and dancing like in a shamanic ritual.

Intensity:
Experiences with strong emotional impact—whether trauma or profound joy—can support transformation and solidify intentions. Sexual orgasms alone or with a consenting partner.

Repetition:
Regular reinforcement of intentions encourages gradual progress, though intense moments may bring immediate shifts. Rituals or routines, for example.

Passive

Authenticity:
Align conscious thoughts and actions with your Soul.

Intentions:
Set clear intentions focussed on growth, collaboration, and reducing entropy.

Selflessness:
Act with genuine regard for others to help reduce entropy. Actions driven by personal gain or ego often yield the opposite effect.

This chapter presents various techniques that connect you to the LCS. Some require active practice, while others can be done passively. It's important to remember that these are tools to get you started. For example, using binaural beats can build confidence in your abilities or confirm that there is more to reality than conventional science suggests.

The elements listed above, categorised into Active and Passive (mechanics), are interwoven throughout the various techniques discussed in this chapter. Depending on the specific practice, certain elements may take precedence. For instance, traditional meditation practices typically emphasise Attention, cultivating deep focus and mindfulness. Conversely, practices like manifesting may require a more profound understanding of one's identity, making Authenticity a more significant factor. It's essential to recognise that these elements are not rigid rules but rather flexible guidelines, as the process of personal growth and transformation is inherently dynamic and evolving.

Ultimately, the goal is to live a good life through increasing authenticity. As you become more authentic, these tools naturally become less relevant, depending on where you are on your path.

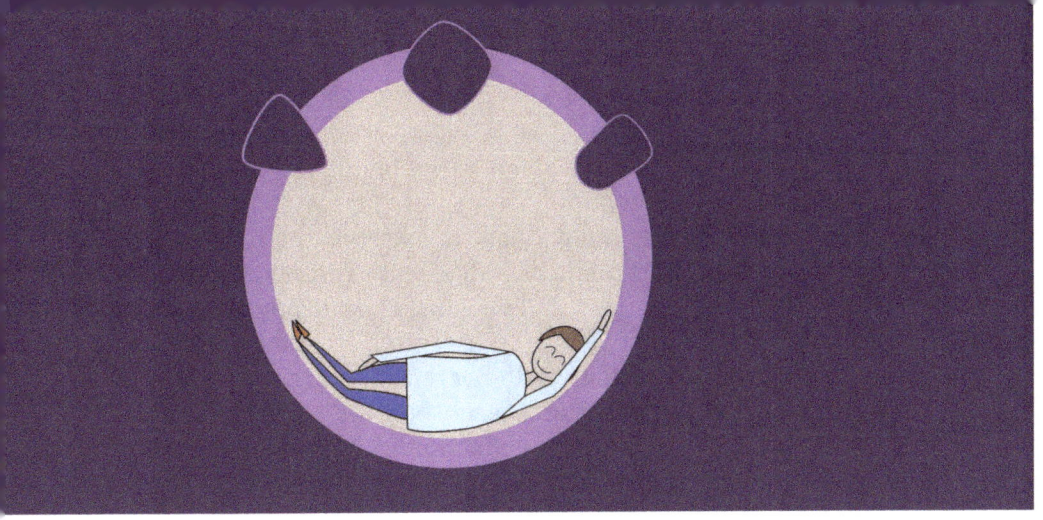

5.3
The Modalities
Ways of Getting There

The LCS suggests that personal growth is reflected in a reduction of entropy—disorder—within the Self. You can observe this process through particular states of Consciousness, such as dreams, fantasies, and meditative states. Each of these states follows different rules from those of everyday waking reality, and each provides insights into one's inner world and mental patterns.

You can achieve meditative or altered states through a range of practices that extend beyond traditional seated meditation. As Grant Cameron discusses in his book Inspired – The Paranormal World of Creativity, you don't have to confine yourself to formal mindfulness exercises or sitting quietly on a meditation cushion. Instead, there are many ways to reach a meditative state by engaging in activities that promote a sense of detachment and inner calm. Think of driving on a monotonous stretch of road, where the steady rhythm of the car can produce effects similar to those of binaural beats; listening to favourite music, which allows the mind to settle into a reflective state; or dancing, where the repetitive movements encourage a feeling of flow and presence. In these instances, the mind shifts naturally into a meditative state, quieting internal chatter and allowing for increased awareness.

In these states, perceptions of time, space, and Self often change. Time may seem to slow, and you may suddenly realise you've been driving for several minutes without actively focussing on the road, immersed in the steady, almost hypnotic sounds of the car. You gain a calm detachment that allows individuals to observe their thoughts and emotions without attachment or judgement. The regular practice of entering these meditative states helps clarify personal motives, increase empathy, and reduce self-centred thinking. Over time, meditative states strengthen self-awareness, align intentions with constructive action, and enhance a sense of interconnectedness with others, all of which support the reduction of entropy within the LCS framework.

Integrating Conscious States
Together, dreams, fantasies, and meditative states serve as channels for accessing less visible areas of Consciousness. By paying attention to the themes and emotions that arise in these states, individuals may uncover hidden motivations, unprocessed fears, and unmet needs. Working through these experiences can support a person's ability to act with authenticity and reduce internal conflict, both of which contribute to lowering entropy.

Progress in reducing entropy can be seen in both personal and social behaviours. High entropy often appears in individuals or groups that emphasise control, strict rules, or dominance, which can create friction and disorder. In contrast, cooperative and considerate actions promote harmonious relationships and smoother interactions. Reducing entropy is not a passive process; it requires active engagement to support oneself and others, but without imposing personal beliefs. By advancing self-awareness, empathy, and collaboration, individuals align more closely with the principles of the LCS, promoting constructive development within themselves and their environments.

Premonitions in the LCS

Premonitions are intuitive insights that enable individuals to access information about probable future events. I see this foresight arise from the LCS, a comprehensive framework that stores and processes a multitude of potential future outcomes. Rather than being mere coincidences or mysterious phenomena, premonitions are grounded in the LCS's structured, probabilistic reality, allowing individuals to perceive high-probability scenarios that may unfold based on current trajectories and underlying probabilities.

The LCS framework proposes a way to interpret premonitions as intuitive glimpses of potential future events that are stored in the system. Rather than being random or mysterious, premonitions are linked to a structured, probabilistic reality.

Future events are not fixed; they exist as a range of possibilities, each carrying its probability. The LCS monitors and recalculates these probabilities as current events unfold. Premonitions are glimpses into these high-probability scenarios, which sometimes become accessible to our awareness without conscious intent.

The LCS holds "probable future" databases, where possible outcomes are stored along with their likelihood. Sometimes, awareness connects with these probable futures, perceiving scenarios that have a significant chance of occurring. This access to high-probability future events forms the basis of premonitions.

Certain individuals might experience premonitions more often due to heightened intuition or natural sensitivity to the LCS's probabilistic information. These individuals may sense probable events, especially when personally or emotionally invested in a specific outcome.

Even when a premonition feels strong, it remains only a probable future rather than a guaranteed outcome. Free will allows choices that can shift the direction of events, alter outcomes and thus changing the probability landscape. Premonitions offer insights into likely scenarios, but these remain open to change based on human decisions.

LCS as a Guide Through Feedback
The LCS functions partially as a feedback mechanism, providing guidance and opportunities for development. Premonitions act as a form of feedback, encouraging individuals to prepare for likely scenarios or make choices that could lead to different outcomes. This guidance aligns with the LCS's broader purpose of nurturing Consciousness and aiding positive growth.

The LCS would not directly steer a person to do certain things, as this goes against its free-will principle. The LCS does have available data streams for the enquiring mind to explore and think of premonitions (passive) or remote viewing (active). See this as giving you more options to consider, broadening your horizon. With this very concrete function built into the LCS, you have more futures to choose from. And as such, you can more precisely direct yourself towards a future that suits you slightly, or fundamentally, better.

In the LCS, premonitions, dreams, and fantasies reveal layers of personal insight that can support a reduction of internal disorder, or entropy. These varied states of Consciousness allow individuals to see more of their inner motivations, fears, and unresolved issues, providing opportunities for genuine self-expression and balanced growth.

The LCS framework posits that Consciousness is the foundation of reality, with each person considered an Individuated Unit of Consciousness (IUoC) that actively shapes their development through free will and intention. Actions guided by cooperation and empathy help lower entropy, creating harmony and strengthening connections with others, while actions based on self-interest or fear tend to increase entropy, leading to disorder and conflict.

Engagement with the LCS requires intentional practices such as setting clear goals, maintaining focus, and acting selflessly. Through these practices, individuals can reinforce lower-entropy behaviours that contribute to both personal growth and more harmonious interactions.

Experiences within the LCS are bound by structured rules of "virtual" physical reality, such as the laws of gravity and time, yet Consciousness itself can extend beyond these boundaries. By reflecting on dreams, fantasies, and meditative states, individuals can find ways to align more closely with the LCS's goals of cooperation and constructive development. This alignment promotes empathy, authenticity, and shared growth, supporting harmony both within and beyond oneself.

Binaural Beats

Binaural beats can be a practical tool for entering meditative states, promoting calm and focus by helping the brain reach a coherent state. While effective for many, they are best used as temporary aids. As I wrote in the chapter The Human Experience, real growth comes not from relying on any single tool, but from developing a flexible approach that balances external aids with inner awareness.

How Binaural Beats Work

Binaural beats are created by playing two slightly different frequencies in each ear. The brain then processes these sounds and perceives a "beat" frequency that equals the difference between the two input frequencies. For example, if one ear hears a tone at 100 Hz and the other at 106 Hz, the listener experiences a beat frequency of 6 Hz. This beat frequency can guide the brain towards synchronisation with the external rhythm, a process known as brainwave entrainment.

Through entrainment, the brain's electrical activity adjusts to align with the beat frequency, often promoting coherence and calm. Different beat frequencies are linked to specific brainwave states; in this case, 6 Hz lies within the theta range (4–8 Hz), commonly associated with deep relaxation and meditative states. Listening to binaural beats tuned to theta frequencies can help the listener enter a calm, focussed mental state more easily, enhancing relaxation and self-awareness. In this synchronised state, many people experience a decrease in mental distraction, increased focus, and a deeper sense of inner stillness.

Experiences

I first experimented with binaural beats myself to see whether they could genuinely deepen meditation. After noticing effects such as enhanced focus, calm, and ease in reaching meditative states, I introduced binaural beats to students. They had mixed responses; some experienced subtle shifts, while others reported most surprising changes.

One student, pregnant at the time, frequently struggled with remembering important tasks for her check-ups, such as forms or test results. After only a few days of listening to binaural beats, she had a vivid dream. In it, she arrived at her appointment only to realise she had forgotten crucial items. The dream allowed her to "go back in time" and repeat the visit until, by the ninth attempt, she remembered everything she needed. When she woke up, she immediately prepared all the necessary items, and the appointment went smoothly. The dream seemed to provide her with a practical solution to an ongoing challenge.

Another student, an exchange student, had an emotional reason for wanting to return to her home country. On the final day of the five-day workshop, after many hours of binaural beats, she planned to catch a specific bus. But a few hours before the journey, she had a strong feeling of taking a later one. Although eager to leave, she decided to wait. The bus she had planned to use was unfortunately involved in a deadly collision. Reflecting on the experience, she wondered how her inner shift might have influenced her decision.

In another instance, I combined binaural beats with an early version of my VR-Lite (my Controlled Remote Viewing hack), a technique aimed at strengthening intuitive perception. One student, already skilled in meditation, managed to describe a target object with extraordinary precision, almost as if he could see it directly. This combination of binaural beats and early CRV exercises seemed to enhance his intuitive abilities, allowing for strikingly accurate perceptions.

Harmonising Tools and Beliefs
While binaural beats can help people enter meditative states, they are not essential. As with formal seated meditation, alternative methods can work just as well. Listening to a favourite song, dancing, or even exercising can lead to similar states of focus and insight. Each person may find different activities that support inner calm and awareness.

However, in a group setting, binaural beats offer a practical advantage. Their neutral, steady sounds avoid the distractions of personal music preferences, creating a consistent environment for all. I sometimes call binaural beats "just boring noise," as their lack of melody helps everyone focus without distraction.

Ultimately, external tools like binaural beats can be useful, but they are not essential. True growth in the Larger Consciousness System lies in balancing reliance on external aids with attachment to internal beliefs. Both ends of this spectrum can limit genuine development—over-dependence on tools can create a sense of dependency, while rigid beliefs can close off openness to new insights.

Real progress happens somewhere between these extremes, where adaptability and awareness guide the way. Using tools like binaural beats can be beneficial, but only if we treat them as temporary supports rather than fixed solutions. Their role is to support personal growth, not to define it. Each person's path is their own, and the most effective growth occurs when we stay flexible, using resources as needed without becoming reliant on any single one.

Manifesting: you get what you need, not what you want.
Manifesting is a technique where you define and focus deeply on what you want in life, and work to bring it into reality. This focus alone exercises your mind, and, regardless of the outcome, has clear benefits already. At first, your thoughts might be broad and undefined, often residing in your subconscious. It's like having a second captain steering the ship when the main captain is asleep.

By clearly defining your goals, you can direct and adjust your emotions, intentions, thoughts, words, and actions in ways that consistently support your path forward. Most noticeable are goals set for this lifetime, but these goals also affect the quality of your Soul over multiple lifetimes. The chapter on Authenticity offers practical guidance on building this alignment, showing how to connect your inner intentions with outward actions and harmonise your conscious (aware) and subconscious (aware) goals with your Soul's desires.

> *Consciousness:*
> *The fundamental entity responsible for awareness, perception, and decision-making. It encompasses both conscious and subconscious awareness, allowing for the experience of reality and interaction with it. Consciousness serves as the source of individual intent, guiding actions and choices within both known and unknown contexts.*
>
> *Conscious Awareness:*
> *The active, deliberate part of the mind that processes information with intention and focus. It engages in immediate thoughts, decision-making, and interactions with the external environment.*
>
> *Subconscious Awareness:*
> *The underlying part of the mind that operates without deliberate focus, storing memories, beliefs, and automatic responses. It influences actions and perceptions indirectly, often without consciously aware recognition.*

Manifesting directs your thoughts, examines deep beliefs, and interacts with your Soul to support or undermine your goals. Your thoughts can be yours, or they can be influenced by others. A significant portion of the beliefs were developed as adaptive mechanisms during childhood, but they may no longer serve their intended purpose. Your Soul has a desire to improve on certain qualities in your lifetime. There are very many possible experiences in which you can work on accomplishing that.

With manifesting you try to bend false, redundant and unwanted beliefs into true, useful and desired beliefs. You do this by examining those beliefs and comparing them with your thoughts. In the exercises, I walk you through this process. Thus, it is necessary to know what you want to think. And here it becomes evident that to know what to think, you need to know what your Soul's purpose is for you in this lifetime.

When your life goals align with both your conscious and subconscious awareness, as well as with your emotions, intentions, thoughts, words, and actions, manifesting becomes almost instinctive. However, many people manage these elements loosely, leading to a disconnect between their goals and their actual course. This disconnect resembles a ship adrift due to a faulty rudder—leaving it vulnerable to external influences and inner conflicts that pull it off course. For a more profound look at these influences and how they challenge our intentions, refer to the chapter on Forces, which explores the dual forces that can strengthen or undermine our direction.

Despite our limited understanding of LCS' inner workings, we can observe outcomes and speculate. Probability (described in Chapter 1) and intention are likely crucial factors. The LCS allows for a range of logical and likely outcomes in any situation for any Soul. You can influence which probabilities become more probable by clearly stating your intentions, such as through an affirmation.

> *Intent*
> *Intent represents the underlying purpose or motivation that drives conscious choices and actions. It reflects the deeper quality of an individual's Consciousness, shaping the direction and impact of their decisions. In the LCS, intent encompasses not just surface-level desires or goals but also the core values, attitudes, and energy that guide interactions and influence probabilities. Intent plays a critical role in the evolution of Consciousness, as focussed and constructive intent aligns with the system's aim to lower entropy, encouraging personal growth, development, and greater harmony within the collective.*

Affirmation:
Affirmations are positive, specific statements that people repeat to themselves to combat negative thoughts or beliefs.
For example, an affirmation like "I wish I had more money" could lead to a misinterpretation by the Soul:
"You wish, so I'll keep you wishing."
"Why does he wish for more money, rather than having it?"
"You want more money. Is 10 cents enough?"

Such misunderstandings arise from ambiguity in the language of affirmation, and detecting these subtleties takes practice. You find exercises and explanations later in this chapter. Crafting a good affirmation also requires you to acknowledge any selfish or negative desires, stemming from deeper fears buried inside you. We all contain both positive and negative traits within us. When you recognise your negative aspects—your "shadow side"—you can begin the work of integrating it into your full identity, rather than rejecting it. Carl Jung speaks about Individuation; I call it becoming Authentic. The positive and negative traits are covered more thoroughly in the chapter on Forces.

Sometimes, events or circumstances can trigger negative thoughts or reactions that shape our perceptions, even if they don't directly change our reality. We share this life with others who each feel, think, and act with varying degrees of influence. It can be tempting to blame or judge others for problems we encounter, yet these reactions primarily shape our perception and experience rather than theirs. Ultimately, we each decide how much of our attention to give to the issues of the wider world. This book serves as a way to offer insights on these concepts while refining my understanding of them.

Core Steps and Ingredients for Manifesting:

Unambiguous Goal, define what you want.
Avoid specifics, let the system find the solution.
State it as if it's already happened.
Keep statements short and focussed.
Be realistic, the system works with probabilities, not magic.
Deep Conviction, know deeply that your goal has already happened.
Practice sensing your body's response to truth and lies.

Use body awareness to verify belief in affirmations.

Repetition, regularly repeating your affirmations is one perspective. Another school of thought suggests being very specific once, and then letting go. I see both sides as being correct, and it probably depends on context.

Bliss and Gratitude, you feel happiness and gratitude as if you've already received what you desire.

If this joy is absent, reassess the goal.

Counter Defeating Thoughts, guard against negativity. Label negative thoughts as lies and reaffirm your goal.

Manifesting outcomes may arrive in unexpected forms. The Soul sends subtle messages, but they won't arrive by mail. Recognising and acting on coincidences, feelings, or ideas speeds up manifesting.

Main Principles of Manifesting

Set a Clear Goal:
Define what you want with clarity. Avoid ambiguity; be specific about your goal.

Use Short, Focussed Statements:
Keep affirmations short and clear. Breakdown complex wishes into separate, simple goals.

Be Realistic:
Set achievable goals. Manifesting operates within the boundaries of probability, not magic. Write affirmations as if you already have what you desire, creating a clear picture for an external, all-powerful source to support and enable.

Manifest Through Affirmation:
Craft clear, simple statements as if the desired outcome is already fully achieved, focussing solely on the final result. Avoid words implying desire or future actions, such as "want" or "will." Expressing gratitude or joy reinforces the feeling that one has already received what they desire, providing a clear directive to a powerful source to enable it in reality.

Test your beliefs:
Train yourself to feel your body's response to truth and lies. Here follows an example of how to train for testing what you think you believe, is what you truly believe.

> *Make up a lie, such as "I have green hair," and silently speak it in your mind. Note any reaction in your body. Where is the reaction, what kind of reaction do you feel, how intense is this reaction?*
>
> *Tell a truth like, "I have black hair," and observe how your body responds differently. Where in the body, how intense, in what for does the reaction come?*
>
> *Repeat until you can reliably recognise how your body feels when something is true versus when it is false.*

When you have gained the experience and confidence to understand where and how your body reacts to your inner truths and lies, utilise this skill when making choices, formulating affirmations, and setting life goals.

Trust the Process: Don't try to control how the outcome will happen. Allow the "system" to find the best way to fulfil your goal. This might come through unexpected events, like meeting the right person at the right moment.

During the day you make choices; each choice has a consequence. The LCS does not force any choice upon you but could nudge the circumstances.

> *You currently hold a routine desk clerk job, but your true passion lies in crafting exclusive travel experiences for couples. Despite the predictability of your current work, you've long envisioned creating bespoke journeys that offer unforgettable moments for partners around the world. Over time, you've planned trips for friends, each met with high praise, reinforcing your belief in your potential as a travel curator. This positive feedback has slowly strengthened your confidence in your skills and passion, leading you to reflect deeply on your aspirations and affirm that this is truly what you want.*
>
> *Now, the LCS has recognised your genuine intentions and drive. The LCS functions as a logical framework aligned with the principles of 'Life on Earth.' Since you haven't identified potential connections in your immediate social or professional circles who could assist you—perhaps because none were evident—the LCS can subtly nudge at the Soul level, helping others recognise the mutual benefit of certain ideas. However, individuals on Earth must also be attuned to the subtle messages their Soul sends. Each person*

ultimately acts based on their intuition, choices, and free will.

Imagine a wealthy client of your husband, who runs a car sales business, invites one of his affluent customers—a business investor and avid collector of exclusive cars—to a luxury car fair. His wife, a lover of early 20th-century Italian sports cars, accompanies him, adding to the occasion. During the event, this client overhears your spouse discussing your aspirations to organise exclusive, romantic trips for couples. To his surprise, he learns that your venture has yet to gain significant traction, despite your dedication to this project alongside your current job. Coincidentally, this client recently invested in a luxury travel startup with plans to offer intimate getaways for couples.

Curious, he scrolls through your social media profiles, where he finds beautifully curated posts about the trips you've organised for friends. The glowing testimonials and personal touch in your posts captivate him, strengthening his confidence in your dedication and talent. Inspired, he feels compelled to explore a potential collaboration.

Buzzing with ideas and opportunities, he contacts the CEO of his new travel agency. Over the phone, he enthusiastically proposes integrating exclusive, romantic trips for couples into their offerings, highlighting the unique market niche and the premium clientele they could attract. His vision aligns perfectly with your skills, and he sees your expertise elevating the agency's high-end reputation.

After the call, he shares his enthusiasm with his wife, who has been admiring a rare sports car at the fair. Upon hearing about your work, she wholeheartedly supports the idea, imagining how easily her friends could book a secret getaway to a fantastic location.

Recognising your dedication and the partnership's potential, he emphasises the need for confidentiality due to the high-profile nature of his clientele. Your spouse, who was previously unaware of the full scope of your venture due to his commitments, now sees the quality of your work and fully supports your aspirations, vouching for your expertise. Consequently, the wealthy client reaches out to you directly. During your meeting, you both quickly recognise the synergy in your visions for creating unparalleled travel experiences.

This convoluted story hopefully illustrates the kinds and number of coincidences that may be necessary for a manifestation to materialise.

Each person has choices (free will), and the more in tune one is with the authentic self, the easier it will be to notice those subtle messages that come to you as intuitions, thoughts, or feelings. Being authentic enhances your ability to notice subtle signals from your Soul, from others, or from the Larger Consciousness System (LCS) at large.

Recognising the best choice largely depends on your ability to listen to your intuition, which manifests both mentally, as a thought, and physically as a sensation in your body, like goose bumps. Start by testing your beliefs to train yourself in recognising how your body responds to truth and lies. First, another quick overview of a manifesting process. I repeat these overviews in slightly different wording and logic, as I want to cover as much diverse ground as possible before getting into the nitty-gritty.

Affirm Completion
Speak and think as if you have already achieved what you want. This creates a feeling of certainty. Try to reach a point where you can vividly feel, smell, hear, taste, and see your manifestation.

Feel Bliss and Gratitude
Imagine you've already received what you're manifesting. Aim to feel genuinely happy and grateful, as if receiving a beautiful gift. It should feel like butterflies in your stomach, joy, or love.

> *Repeat:*
> *Often: repeat your affirmations regularly, as often as you comfortably can. Ideally, your realistic and positive attitude and mindset become your default, negating the need for active manifesting.*
>
> *Once: In the context of using manifesting techniques for magical practices, you invoke the 'magical phrase' and let go. This could mean you stop thinking about the phrase, burn the paper it is written on, or something equivalent.*
>
> *Hold a Strong Belief:*
> *Cultivate a deep and unwavering feeling that your goal has already been fulfilled.*
>
> *Re-evaluate Misaligned Goals:*
> *If you don't feel happy while visualising your goal, consider if the goal is right for you. If it were aligned, it would bring a sense of joy.*

Believe in the System:
If you doubt that manifesting works, remind yourself that the system operates by aligning events and people around you, not by performing miracles. It opens doors, but you must walk through them. As the saying goes, "You cannot win the lottery without buying a ticket."

Counter Defeating Thoughts:
Negative thoughts undermine manifesting and can be combated with practice. Strengthen your "manifesting muscle" by recognising defeating thoughts as false, saying, "that's a lie," or any other simple, powerful phrase that resonates. Then, repeat your affirmation with conviction.

The Power of Belief in Shaping Reality and the Future

Beliefs about oneself and the future play a critical role in shaping actions and interactions. A positive self-image—seeing oneself as healthy, happy, or capable—naturally encourages confident behaviour, which others often respond to positively. This mindset helps nurture stronger connections and better experiences with those around you. When people feel assured of their worth or potential, they engage more openly and create a cycle that reinforces these qualities.

Conversely, a negative self-image reflects in actions and interactions, which may lead to a cycle of self-doubt and discouragement. This negativity can limit the scope of your interactions and cloud how you perceive opportunities, making it difficult to engage fully with others and hindering personal development.

The beliefs we hold about our future also affect our present-day actions. When a person envisions a successful, fulfilling future, they are more likely to take proactive steps—embracing new opportunities, taking calculated risks, and investing time and energy in meaningful projects and relationships. A positive outlook attracts support, creating a network of allies who can assist in moving closer to personal goals.

In contrast, expecting a challenging or bleak future can lead to caution and reservation. People who anticipate difficulty may withdraw from risks or hold back in relationships, fearing disappointment or failure. This restrained approach often leads to isolation, as others sense hesitance and may disengage in turn. Over time, this outlook can become self-reinforcing, reducing positive connections and limiting pathways to growth.

An example
In the example below, I walk you through practical steps and reflections so you can practise affirmations and manifesting.

Creating a clear, specific affirmation for financial abundance involves progressively refining vague statements into a precise, achievable goal. This process clarifies intent and addresses potential self-doubt or limiting beliefs. Let's take the example of someone starting with the affirmation: "I want to be financially secure." We'll improve this sentence in stages, working towards a final statement that is confident, abundant, and worry free.

Step 1: State Your Affirmation Out Loud

Action:
Say, "I would like to be financially secure."

Example:
By saying the affirmation out loud, listen for any words or phrases that sound weak, uncertain, or too broad.

Weak Starting Sentence:
"I want to be financially secure."

Issue:
This sentence is vague and future-focussed. It expresses a desire but lacks specifics about what "financially secure" actually means.

Goal:
Speaking the affirmation can help you identify areas that feel too open-ended.

Reflect on Potential Discomfort or Self-Limiting Fears:
Notice if the term "financially secure" brings up any doubts or resistance. For example, you might feel uncertain about whether you're allowed to claim financial security fully

fearing it might sound "greedy" or "selfish". Acknowledging any discomfort here can reveal limiting beliefs.

Step 2: Identify the Core Desire

Action:
Ask yourself, "What does financial security actually mean to me?"

Example:
If financial security means having a steady income, being free of debt, or having savings, specify these aspects.

Slightly Improved Sentence:
"I am financially secure."

Issue:
Though in the present tense, this phrase is still ambiguous. "Financially secure" can mean different things to different people, making the affirmation difficult to visualise or measure.

Goal:
Clarify what "financial security" means to you personally.

Reflect on Potential Discomfort or Self-Limiting Fears:
As you narrow down your desire, you may feel hesitant to fully define it. Fears of appearing "too ambitious" can sometimes keep us from clear expression. Recognising these feelings helps you address them so you can refine the affirmation confidently.

Step 3: Replace General Words with Concrete Terms

Action:
Replace vague terms like "financially secure" with specific, measurable outcomes.

Example:
Change "financially secure" to "earn enough money to live comfortably."

Even More Improved Sentence: "I earn enough money to live comfortably."

Issue:
This adds some clarity, but terms like "enough money" and "live comfortably" are still open to interpretation. This step still needs practical detail to make it actionable.

Goal:
Ensure that every key term in the affirmation has a clear, personal meaning.

Reflect on Potential Discomfort or Self-Limiting Fears:
If specifying amounts feels uncomfortable, it might be due to a fear of committing to clear goals. Addressing these feelings can help make the affirmation more precise.

Step 4: Ask, "What Does This Look Like?" for Each Key Word

Action:
For each term of the affirmation, ask yourself, "If this were real, what would it look like in my life?"

Example:
For "enough money" and "live comfortably", imagine practical elements like a budget or a savings plan.

A further Refined Sentence: "I earn a stable income that covers my monthly expenses and allows me to save."

Issue:
This version brings in the idea of a stable income and covering expenses, but it still lacks specifics for true clarity.

Goal:
Visualising each term removes any remaining ambiguity, giving a clear picture of what "financial security" means in daily life.

Reflect on Potential Discomfort or Self-Limiting Fears:
Visualising each part may reveal fears around budgeting or tracking savings. Recognising these fears helps you build an affirmation that reflects your true goals.

Step 5: Transform into an Abundance-Focussed Affirmation

Action:
With a clearer sense of your financial goals, shift the language to reflect a state of abundance, emphasising security and ease.

Example:
Transform the affirmation into: "I live in an abundance of financial wealth and have no worries about anything finance-related."

Issue:
This final affirmation expresses both financial stability and freedom from financial concerns. It uses present-tense language that reflects confidence and aligns with the concept of living in a continuous state of abundance.

Goal:
Complete the shift from a wishful statement to a clear expression of financial abundance and peace of mind.

As you continue to work with the affirmation, notice any physical or emotional responses when you repeat it daily. Discomfort or resistance may indicate underlying fears or doubts about your worthiness for financial freedom. For example, if you feel tightness or unease, ask if you truly believe in the abundance you're affirming, or if lingering doubts remain. Recognising and addressing these feelings is essential to fully embracing the affirmation.

With this affirmation refined as "I live in an abundance of financial wealth and have no worries about anything finance-related", you now have a statement that reflects both security and a mindset free of worry. This final version should feel empowering, aligning clearly with your goals and bringing you closer to the reality you wish to create.

But does this work?
If you picked up the last affirmation "I live in an abundance of financial wealth and have no worries about anything finance-related" and repeat that, the chances are not much will change for you. The process is more important than the sentence. Perhaps even more disappointing, at the end of this long chapter, you do not even need an affirmation.

The LCS has not evolved to create "stuff" for incarnated souls in the "Life on Earth" simulation. Manifesting is a process of you becoming aware of your beliefs and expressions, and adjusting them to suit your goals better, and those of your Soul. You need to become aware of coincidences, opportunities, signs, and act upon them. Therefore, you need courage to find out what you want, and consequently face yourself, the good and bad.

And when you have done so, you need the courage to act, to become your authentic self.

Remote Viewing

Throughout my life, I have had experiences that I could not explain to conventional, materialistic sciences apart from calling them coincidences or imagination. Here, I speak about premonitions or events where I peeked into another reality. Over time, I was able to understand which emotional states, events, or locations could increase the likelihood of such occurrences.

For example, moments of deep sadness or intense bliss have been times when I was mindful or my mind was in a meditative state—engaging in something repetitive or keeping my conscious awareness occupied. In such states, other data or information about future events—things happening far away, about which I could not have any knowledge, or occurring in another reality—could be received.

> One of these events was very traumatic for me. My grandmother, who was like a mother to me, had started to develop a form of Alzheimer's or dementia. One night, only three days before my father was to pick her up and bring her to our home, where she could live with more care and safety, my grandmother went out on a stormy and rainy night. That night, in my dream, I saw her walking off the path next to a little white metal bridge that crosses a small canal, common in the Dutch landscape. Moments later, I saw her lying in the canal, face down. Shortly after, she was picked up by a black funeral hearse pulled by clichéd angels that seriously

> looked as if they had just left a Christmas tree. They smiled, which I found disturbing and interpreted as them being mean to me. The next morning, I told this to my mother, who didn't want to hear any more of it.

> My grandmother was missing for more than a day until someone found her deceased in the water next to the little metal bridge.

By that time, I had learned to keep most of those kinds of experiences to myself. In my early youth, these kinds of experiences, when shared with my family, were ridiculed if not worse. But the above was too important not to share; no one believed me, of course. It was only when my grandmother was found that my mother finally made a comment that seemed to acknowledge her existence. However, by that time, she was already overcome with sadness.

I am not the only one with these kinds of experiences, nor the only one who decided to keep silent about them. What I have done differently with my spouse, children and friends is listening and ask a few questions. The way I listen to others and ask questions is like interrogating myself. I devised a guerrilla strategy for interpreting my dreams and flashes of insight. The core of this strategy was to elevate the information to a higher level of abstraction, thereby removing emotional prejudices. For instance, if in a dream I saw someone I know doing something, I would take off their "mask" and look at what they represent. Was this person female, or male, or a non-human entity? Was the person friendly or not? Was it me, my feminine or masculine side, my anima, or animus? My attempts were to stand back and be an observer rather than a participant.

Regardless of my desire and attempts to have trust and faith in what I saw, heard, felt, or observed, lifelong repression had taken its toll. I was unsure if what I observed had any reality to it or was merely my imagination. And imagination, I have plenty of that. But there is a distinct difference between making things up for some reason and receiving information out of the blue without asking for it or intending to use it. Then, a good friend asked if I would like to join him for a Controlled Remote Viewing (CRV) workshop. I was familiar with remote viewing and had read quite a few articles and papers and watched many videos on the topic. Remote viewing fascinated me tremendously!

So my answer was, "No."

I was scared—scared that after all these years, my experiences were nothing more than my imagination running circles around me and that during this workshop, I would be unmasked. Negative emotions from my youth, which had gradually accumulated, began to surface, and in fact, I nearly panicked. How could I get underneath this suggestion to join the workshop?

After many attempts to resist the invitation, my friend offered to pay for the entire workshop, which was a significant sum of money. There was no way I could decline such a generous offer, so there I went. Long story short, I had a blast, and my confidence shot through the roof. My fears were unfounded.

But the important thing I learned was how to structure the process. As I had attempted to do with my guerrilla tactics, I learned to start from a high level of abstraction and gradually add details.

What is Remote Viewing?
Before I participated in the CRV workshop, I had some familiarity with the various definitions and approaches regarding CRV. In fact, there were fierce battles about which process was the best, the truest to the originator, and all kinds of disagreements.

The 'father of remote viewing' was often named as Ingo Swann, either in combination with the people at Stanford Research Institute (SRI) like Hal Puthoff and Russell Targ. There were many more people involved, some names only now beginning to surface. There was undoubtedly a lot of cloak-and-dagger going on in those circles, and this is of no interest to me. But among all those people, I had an instant click with Ingo Swann.

It turns out he was like me, a Virgo/Rooster (astrology), a thinker and ponderer, an artist with a public and private side, and of course, gifted in the field of CRV and interacting with the LCS. Now, to make this clear, I do not compare myself with him in terms of abilities. I consider him much more advanced, and it is also not my goal to do what he had done. I have my path.

These days, I observe the CRV field with a keen eye but do not participate. I use my principles of authenticity to integrate my abilities—you have them too, to varying degrees—into my daily and nightly routines. As CRV is a valuable tool to learn to structure insights that you might get, I therefore want to give you some grip on what it is.

Out of the many definitions you see here, something Tom Campbell might say, and what photographer, graphic designer, and remote viewer Dan Smith writes.

> *Tom:*
> Getting data (and then putting it into, for example, words and images).
>
> *Daz:*
> Remote Viewing is the trained ability to acquire accurate direct knowledge not available to the ordinary physical senses, of locations, things, and events — these are distant in time or space from the Remote Viewer and can be in the past, present, or future.

Neither one of them opens up to you, I suppose, unless you are already familiar with CRV. Below is an attempt to present a reasonably agreed-upon structure of a remote viewing process. There will be variations among viewers, omitting steps or adding steps. But for you, the reader, this overview below should communicate that CRV is structured and not a vague process.

Remote Viewing is like taking off the layers of an onion, one layer at a time. RV is not guessing neither channeling nor being a clairvoyant. In fact, the best results in my classes and workshops were with people who actually didn't care that much if RV worked or not, but wanted to give is a shot. The people with the least useful results were those who were on either end of the spectrum of strong belief.

> *Task Initiation:*
> Someone (a client) somewhere has a desire or need to know something specific about an event, location, person, and so forth (things), or something more general.
>
> *Task Definition:*
> This desire or need is put into words, excluding ambiguity and limiting the number of 'things'. This description of need or desire is then called a task.

Task Assignment:
This task is then given by the client to someone, often some tasker. In some instances, the tasker receives the task in, for example, a closed envelope and does not open it, remaining 'blind to the task'. Alternatively, the tasker reads the tasks.

Code Attachment:
Regardless of being blind or not, the tasker then attaches a random code, let's say 8 digits, to the task. This is also called a coordinate.

Viewer Selection:
The tasker selects viewers that could be suitable for the task at hand and only sends them the random code, for example, an 8-digit number.

Viewer Reception:
The viewer receives the random code and begins to work.

Preparation:
Each viewer has a preferred method or methods to get started. Some meditate, some use binaural beats, some do nothing.

Documentation Tools:
The viewer can work from a whiteboard, sheets of paper, or other materials to write and draw on. Documenting the process is essential.

Initial Setup:
The random code is added, often on the top left of the paper or whiteboard. The date and place are at the top right. Occasionally, the viewer's name or another identifier is included.

Recording Impressions:
From now onwards, all impressions are noted and written (or drawn) from top to bottom, and the pages are numbered. The order is important for later review.

Ideogram Drawing:
The first impression, an ideogram, is drawn, typically with one stroke of a pen. It could be fluid, jagged, or any combination imaginable. The first impression is what the viewer receives as data or information and tries to interpret in this reality.

Analytical Overlay (AOL):
Occasionally, the first impression is spot on, and if the viewer has a clear impression, this is written down as an AOL, which stands for Analytical Overlay. This means that the accumulated data triggered the more awake, conscious mind to make a guess. This might be right or wrong, but the viewer needs to distinguish between guesses and data.

Glyph Identification:
The viewer begins to write down glyphs that represent high-level categories of our reality. I name a few: man-made, energy and movement.

Data Expansion:
The viewer adds more data, and for example, a landscape begins to take on characteristics such as hot, sandy and dusty. Depending on the task and its environment, the viewer begins to describe this environment.

Concept Formation:
The longer in the process, the more data flows in, clearer shapes form, and concepts begin to emerge.

Comprehensive Documentation:
Everything is written down and, in some cases, spoken and recorded.

AOL Labelling:
Sudden flashes of what the target might be, are jotted down and labelled "AOL".

Picture Emergence:
As the process unfolds, a picture emerges, often including the surroundings, activities, players (like humans involved), emotions, smells, and feelings.

Sensory Representation:
The five senses are also represented in the discovery. Some viewers recognise smells more, sooner, or in more detail than others, and the same goes for the other senses.

Target Recognition:
At some stage in the process, the viewer might begin to recognise what the target is about. Here, the viewer needs to stay away from fantasy and stay close to the data. Fantasy shall later prove to lead to off-target directions or simply prove the plan wrong.

Tasker Interaction:
The tasker, if present during the process, might ask, for example, 'look to the right' or 'enter that building that you just described'. Essential is that the tasker does not plant suggestions.

Session Termination:
When suggestions are planted and the viewer starts to use the mind and begins to 'think', the session needs to end. At that stage, guessing happens. The viewer might have luck or be right, though this is outside the scope of the remote viewing process.

Result Submission:
When the viewer cannot add anything more, the whole documented process is handed in to the tasker.

Result Review:
The tasker either reviews the results or does this in collaboration with the client.

Validation:
In some cases, often in the testing phases, the results are handed over to a team or 'judge' that has no prior knowledge of the task. This team or judge describes the findings and then compares them to the original task. This could provide some insight into how accurate the viewer was.

The above linear process could be reshuffled in places, and some items could be added, altered, or removed. Some qualified remote viewers might explode in anger as well. But here you have a decent overview that is close to my experiences and that of the hundreds of processes I have heard about through discussions.

RV-Lite

Back in 2017, I conducted a workshop titled 'Where Do Ideas Come From' (Ajatus) at the Department of Sculpting, Aalto University in Helsinki, Finland. The audience comprised primarily art and sculpting students in the early stages of their studies. I aimed to communicate the difference between ideas and good ideas, how being authentic helps you find good ideas, and how I define authenticity. Later in this chapter, I discuss how to use a simplified version of one of these tools called remote viewing, which I refer to as RV-lite lacking a better term.

Ideas and Good Ideas

After an introduction, my workshop began with the question: What is a good idea? Or what does it mean to have a good idea?

I collected the answers and wrote the results on the blackboard. It proved remarkably difficult for the students to define an idea, and none of the answers explained what a good idea was.

My definition is that an idea is a mental understanding, thought, or notion that exists or is generated by the mind. It is crucial to note the 'mental' and 'mind' aspects. The definition of a good idea incorporates the mind and mental aspects but adds three distinct attributes: time, emotions, and audience.

But how do we define 'idea' and 'good idea'? Throughout my thinking and workshops, I have developed these general notions of how I perceive 'ideas' and 'good ideas'.

> *Idea:*
> An idea is a mental concept or thought that represents a potential course of action, solution, or creative notion.
>
> *Good Idea:*
> A good idea is a mental concept or thought that represents a practical, effective, and beneficial course of action, solution, or creative notion.

The main difference between an 'idea' and a 'good idea' is that a good idea adds value, is beneficial, or has a positive impact.

These three attributes I added make all the difference and bring us to this twilight zone or fringe area of our shared reality, which is perceived by our five senses and Consciousness. The main difference between an idea and a good idea is that a good idea is well received (emotion) by one or more individuals (audience) in the future (time). The better an idea is received by as large a group as possible in the future, the difference between a good idea and a great idea becomes evident.

I consider time the least interesting attribute. As long as the positive reception by an audience occurs in the future, it suffices. What is more fascinating is the intensity of the emotions and the size of the audience, with many people giving their focussed attention. Additionally, regularly engaging with the idea (repetition) helps reinforce its presence and impact. A good idea occurs when, in the future, as large an audience as possible displays increasingly positive responses based on an artefact that has come into existence through mental and physical processes.

The question now remains: how do you obtain a good idea? In the following section, I present a simplified form of remote viewing that can be used as-is or serve as the basis for your tools. I recommend the latter, like modifying existing tools and creating your help you to understand more deeply the fundamentals that make such tools work. Furthermore, the process of quieting your mind, allowing data to come in, and writing it down helps you become more authentic. Becoming increasingly authentic enhances your ability to quiet your mind and receive useful data and information.

Exploring the Future with My RV-Lite Method

Here, I introduce a variation of my method for exploring the near future, and perhaps the more distant future. The LCS structures the linear time future as probabilities. Some events are very likely, while many are not. The closer you are to the present moment, the more accurately you can predict what is probable, even certain. Additionally, we have laws such as gravity. For example, when you hold a pencil in front of you, up in the air, with the intent of releasing it, it is extremely likely that the pencil will move towards the ground under normal circumstances.

Estimating exactly what will happen in 10 minutes is much more challenging in everyday situations. I exclude scenarios such as being locked up, being asleep, or being in a meditative state, and so forth. As you can imagine, estimating what exactly happen one year from now is still more challenging, to put it mildly. The LCS allows you to extract future data as probabilities. With the RV-Lite approach, I want you to have a chance to experience this. The main point, though, is that you learn to differentiate between your intuition—subtle data or information that comes through—and your mind doing the thinking and guessing.

Additionally, let go of fear. I had tremendous fear of failing to join the CRV workshop. These days, I shrug my shoulders, as I no longer care whether I get it right. My focus is on growing to become more and more authentic, and being in touch with what I truly believe, think, feel, and desire is most important. Being able to differentiate between my intuition and thoughts that are influenced by others is crucial in this process.

In the instructions below, I have two entities: the tasker and the viewer, or viewers. You can use these instructions to experiment with a group of people, either as a tasker or as one of the viewers.

Materials:
Gather the following materials: folded A4 paper, writing instruments, and access to an RV image database. Set up your environment by finding a quiet, distraction-free space to help you focus and think clearly.

The Flow:
Take your A4 paper and divide it in half by drawing a line or folding it. On the left side, write down thoughts that come from rational thinking or conscious guessing. On the right side, record 'out of the blue' or intuitive thoughts that emerge spontaneously without logical reasoning. Begin the binaural beats session to relax your mind. Now that you have started to listen to the binaural beats, try to relax and avoid thinking. Thoughts will come to your mind anyway, but do not encourage them by, for example, starting a dialogue with yourself. Play binaural beats and let your thoughts flow naturally for 10 minutes. Write down or draw anything that comes through your intuition, or clear thoughts like a guess of what the photo might be about.

Write down any sensations that you feel, like sudden shivers of cold or waves of heat. If you 'hear' sounds, describe them, such as 'bells ringing'. If the word 'red' suddenly comes to your mind, write it down on the right side. If you think it might be a 'red apple', put that on the left side. The idea is to gather anything that pops up, whether as an intuition or a thought.

10 Minutes Later:
After the 10 minutes are over, put down your pen or pencil and turn your paper around or put it away. Avoid any temptation to add something. The goal is not to guess the image or have it perfectly correct, but to learn to distinguish

between your intuitive voice and your rational mind, which includes fears, desires, and more.

What you learn over time is to recognise which kind of data comes more easily to you, more clearly or first. Some people see things, while others first get sounds or very distinct smells. The development of these senses increases by putting in the hours. The more you practise, the richer the data set becomes, and the better you can describe the target image.

Selecting the target:
Next, the tasker selects a random number by picking a number between 1 and 100 randomly. You can find plenty of random number generator websites and applications for your smartphone. The tasker uses the chosen number to select a corresponding image from an online remote viewing image database.

If you, the tasker, do not have access to such an image database, ask a trusted person (non-viewer) to select an image for you after the 10 minutes have passed. You can of course skip step 5. It is important not to get disturbing images, as those do not help your process. A remote viewing image database has hundreds of 'safe images'—images that are distinct and do not relate to disturbing events, scenery, or people.

Analyse:
Now that you have found the target image, set it aside after you have done the writing and drawing, and begin to analyse your data. You can also analyse your data first; it should not matter. Do what feels most natural to you.

I like to organise in various ways, depending on the context in which I conduct these sessions. I enjoy experimenting, testing, and trying different ideas. For example, you could analyse the data according to the five senses: seeing, hearing, feeling, smelling, and asking. Another option is to stay closer to the traditional CRV protocol. If you choose that, use these categories: man-made, natural, energy and motion, gas, objects, vegetation, life, water, and land. But, as with so much, feel free to include high-level categories that make sense to you. Time will show you which are beneficial and which are less so.

Collect your data by gathering all the entries from the right side of the A4 and placing your data in the most relevant category. We'll leave the left side data for now. Once you have categorised all the data (words and drawings), look at the target photo. After doing so, judge which data relates to the target photo. When you are serious about practising any form of remote viewing, I suggest having another person judge the work.

Judging:
The next step is to validate or judge the degree to which a word or drawing is part of how you would describe the target. Imagine you have two boats at sea, with fog and cold weather. In your data, you have 'water' and 'cold'. These fit very well, as you began to describe the environment. Next, you find in your 'smell' category the words oil, salt, and wine. Oil and salt can easily be matched. Oil is perhaps part of the boat, and salt could very well relate to the sea

It is not necessary to have an inner conversation about whether salt could be a pack of salt inside the boat or what type of salt it is about. And the wine? In this example, it makes no sense that you would smell wine. Perhaps, wine is a substitute for "something sour" or "some red drinkable liquid", or some thought that came into the process.

Stay high-level and apply a broad brushstroke attitude. This RV-lite exercise cannot be compared to a highly detailed, 'real' RV session.

Conversely, water, cold, salt, wine, and oil would not give you the descriptions of two boats at sea. You might have received larger chunks of information, like 'boat' or 'windy weather at sea'.

Variations:
Next, check how the data from the other side of the A4 matches. In every class I taught, and the class had about 20 or more participants, there were one or two people who had the data flipped—the intuitive data was on the left side instead of the right, and vice versa. Even though they understood the division of the A4 and the purpose of the course, regardless, check if the 'thinking' side has 'hits' or data that matches what you see in the photo.

The purpose is not to get a perfect hit, but to teach you the distinction between thinking and intuition, to help you overcome self-doubt and fears of failure. This exercise also teaches you that we can perceive data from the future and describe it, albeit in a fragmented manner.

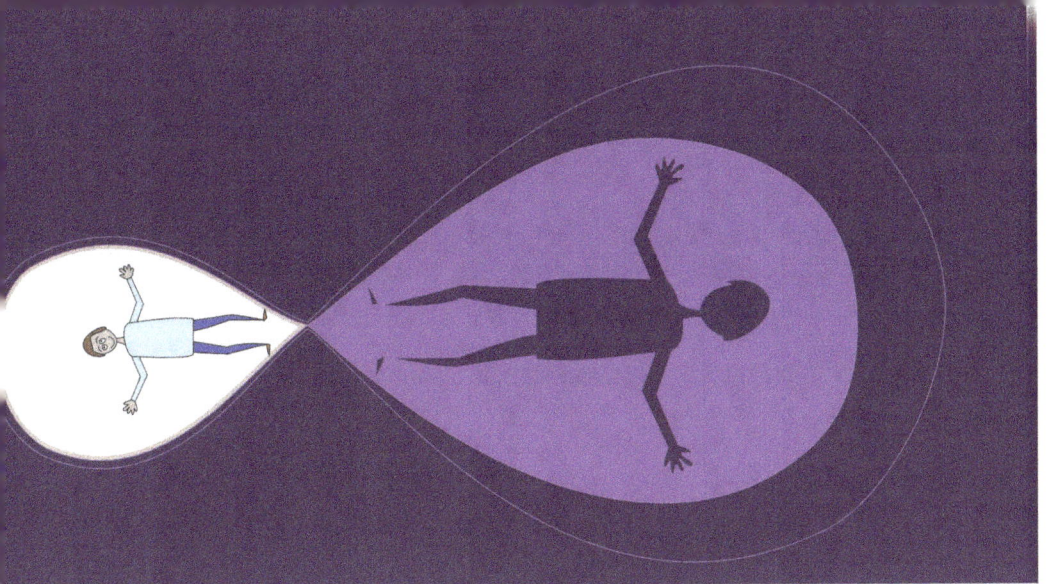

6
Authenticity

Designing Your Life: The Blueprint for Authenticity

After almost ten years (2006-2016) trying to start a meaningful internet service, I reached a breaking point. It became clear that the project needed someone with different qualities. This tiring period was finally ending, making way for a big change and deep thinking about why I struggled for so long. During this tiring period, I made lists of my failures, misunderstandings, naivety, and stubbornness, along with moments of clarity and good ideas. These lists showed a mix of good and bad experiences that stayed with me. While I couldn't change the past, I could influence the future. As feelings of anger, frustration, and disappointment began to fade, I looked honestly at myself and asked:

> *"If you think you are such a good designer, why can't you design your life?"*

As I prepared for a workshop and a series of talks at the Art Academy in Tallinn in 2016, I took this detailed list of the ups and downs of my youth, student time and career, and mapped them onto a timeline. I noticed that my successes and failures corresponded with periods of happiness and frustration. I realised that most of the good decisions I made were aimed at helping others, which brought me a lot of satisfaction. This is a common theme in my life and although this sounds laudable, I had gone too far.

> *I recall a parent-teacher meeting at my elementary school, where the teacher informed my parents, while I was present, that if Jeroen devoted more time to his tasks and less to helping others, he would achieve excellent marks in his report card.*

> *During my high school years, I took over the art class and taught my classmates for a few weeks. The teacher asked me to do this because she saw that I could draw enough well and had the ability to motivate even the most challenging and demotivated students to achieve satisfactory to good results.*

> *My spouse would occasionally tease me about starting a business called Jesus Oy (Oy is a limited company in Finnish), as I'm always eager to help others.*

All too often, the satisfaction of helping others has come at my expense. It may have benefited others, but at the cost of my well-being and, in some cases, that of my immediate family. This insight led me to examine what hinders my happiness and what causes me to make poor choices. These choices, whether big or small, affected my happiness, productivity, and sense of being true to myself.

Becoming authentic is an ongoing process and won't end. There are always new discoveries of old coping strategies or masks that are holding me back. The idea of traumatic experiences causing bodily ailments, as theorised by Ryke Geerd Hamer in his German New Medicine, makes sense to me in the light of and the role of trauma in behaviour and human development within the LCS. I hope to find time to explore this relationship in another book that focusses on health and the LCS.

For this book, I've included exercises to assist you in this journey towards true self-discovery. But first I will share my definition of authenticity and my personal formula for living authentically:

> **Authenticity**
> *Authenticity is a state of alignment where your intentions, emotions, and expressions align with your Soul's deepest values and truths. This alignment is guided by conscious awareness and self-acceptance. It includes emotional unity, the capacity to meaningfully engage with others and society, and the preparedness to navigate external influences while staying true to your innate essence.*

Becoming Authentic is the ongoing process of aligning one's conscious awareness, emotions, thoughts, words, and actions with one's true Self. This journey requires the courage to confront personal fears and societal expectations, navigating desires and anxieties to make conscious choices that genuinely reflect the essence of who you are. Embracing authenticity leads to significant personal growth, improved well-being, and cultivates deeper connections with others. While this honesty may sometimes be met with discomfort by those who prioritise social harmony, prioritising Self-love and genuine experiences ultimately enhances one's sense of Self and positively influences how others perceive you. Recognising that achieving full alignment is a challenging journey that may not be fully realised within a single lifetime, authenticity is measured by how closely your actions in this lifetime correspond to your Soul.

If you enter this life directly from "Soul-land", why do you become misaligned?

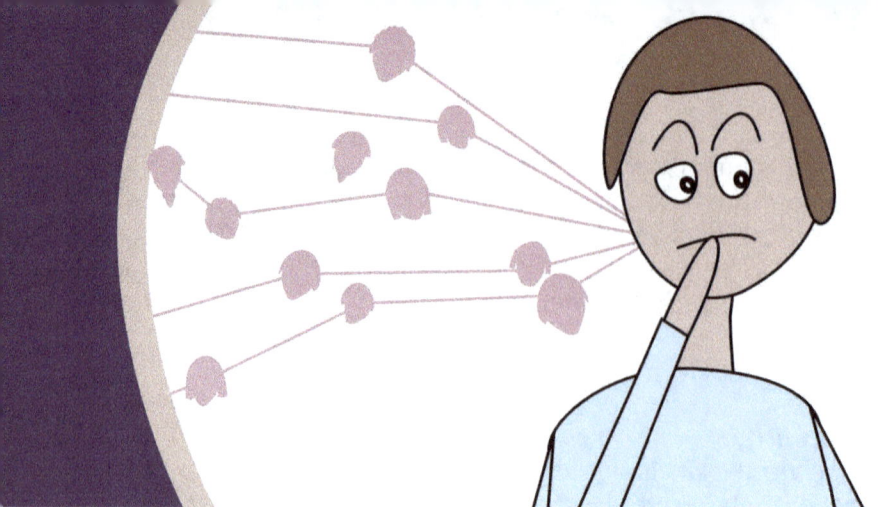

6.1
Overcoming Masks and Embracing Growth
Overcoming shame

From the moment upon arrival and onwards through life, many and diverse forces affect you. An intense event, such as a mother-child separation on the first day of kindergarten, can lead to a traumatic experience. When you feel abandoned, you need to find a way to cope. This may involve trying to fit in with other children, which requires pretending everything is okay.

Now, there are many variations on this theme, but let's focus on the given example. When you try to be someone else, replacing your sad, helpless you with a happier one, your unconscious awareness creates an updated version of the "abandonment part". This allows you to behave differently when you feel abandoned, such as smiling and joking, or becoming angry and isolating. Traumatic events, both big and small, often happen during adolescence, and if a new mask is needed, your unconscious awareness creates it.

And this is how gradually your unconscious awareness replaces the original parts of itself with new parts that cope better with the traumas, or situations that resemble the traumatic experience. However, once some new parts are no longer necessary, since the actual traumatic event no longer occurs, they begin holding you back. When the unconscious awareness receives a signal reminding it of a

Authenticity

past trauma, the mask comes out. Your behaviour changes, even though there is no real need. The consequences can be many, including a distorted self-image, poor interactions with others, and overall dysfunctional habits.

Now, you can find those masks, face them, and use the best qualities of them, as not everything was bad to begin with. This you can do in various forms and I know my method best, so I tell about that one. In a way, you will be travelling back in time, remembering certain events, then linking them to the mask you have created. In Jungian psychology, the shadow resembles a mask, or a collection of masks. I call the collection of masks and the connected emotions, thoughts, words and actions your "secret life". The life that you want to hide from others, even from yourself. I will now concentrate on the journey of becoming true to oneself and leave the complex world of traumas and a fractured ego mind behind.

Becoming more authentic is a gradual process. It involves connecting your values and beliefs with your actions and words. This means recognising how emotions, intentions, thoughts, and actions interact to shape each other. An emotion can lead to an intention, which influences your thoughts, and those thoughts guide your actions. Your actions, in turn, may cause emotions in yourself or others, continuing this cycle.

Being authentic and growing as a person is not about making simple, clear-cut life choices. Simple choices, such as wanting to take a glass of water, are not the kinds of choices I speak about. Life rarely gives us clear "yes" or "no" answers, or choices that are purely "good" or "evil." While there are certainly times of extremes, most choices fall somewhere in the middle. Each decision you make is influenced by intentions, circumstances, and other factors that are not always immediately clear.

> *Imagine you agree to take on an extra project at work. On the surface, this choice seems positive—it shows dedication and could lead to new opportunities. But if your decision is actually driven by a fear of disappointing others or a need to feel valued, it may not truly align with what you want. Alternatively, consider turning down the project to focus on something more meaningful to you. This choice might feel "wrong" if it disappoints others or seems risky, but it could lead to greater personal growth and help you set healthy boundaries.*

Being authentic means recognising and accepting this range of motivations, understanding that most choices cannot be classified as purely right or wrong. Often, our ideas about what is acceptable are shaped by cultural, social, or personal beliefs. But true growth involves looking beyond these labels and reflecting on the reasons behind each choice, understanding that motivations can be complex and mixed.

This is where the concept of spectrum-duality comes into play. By recognising that choices often involve a blend of intentions, we can see that opposing forces—like growth and stagnation, or love and fear—exist on a spectrum rather than as simple opposites. True growth lies in navigating this spectrum and finding balance, rather than following rigid beliefs or external doctrines. Simply becoming aware of these nuances is already a step forward, and this chapter offers exercises to help you examine your motivations and navigate choices with greater clarity.

Smaller steps
Seeing growth as a spectrum-duality makes it easier to take action. When we consider growth to be an "all or nothing" choice—either "good" or "bad"—the decision to move in any direction can feel daunting, often leading to hesitation or delay. This approach creates a high threshold that can prevent us from making choices about our own authentic growth.

In contrast, a spectrum view allows for smaller, gradual steps. Progress does not require dramatic change, but instead can be built up steadily with smaller actions that feel more achievable. This way, you can make small shifts towards growth without the pressure of major change.

For instance, if you want to be more open with others, you don't need to start by sharing deeply personal thoughts. Instead, you could first focus on expressing simple opinions with close friends or trusted people in low-stake situations. As you become more comfortable with these smaller acts of openness, you will likely build confidence, making it easier to bring this honesty into more challenging situations over time. Each small step contributes to overall growth, allowing you to develop gradually and sustainably.

Taking small, manageable steps along this spectrum reduces the pressure and makes authentic growth more accessible.

Warning on Authenticity

Becoming authentic doesn't necessarily mean you need to fully open up on all occasions to all people or entities. Ideally, we would live in a world of harmony and love, but we don't. Yes, the LCS might very well be geared to promoting love, and the afterlife is also all-loving perhaps. But here you are, experiencing a physical reality—harsh at times—with its rules. I so often hear, "we are all love," perhaps, but not in this reality called Life on Earth.

The idea of acting "kind and loving" is another coping mechanism. Acting like that can help you to recognise the positive effect it has on you and others. But that remains effects and does not (yet) come from the authentic you. You might as well need admiration from your peers and now use the mask for "being enlightened".

> *"If you are truly enlightened, you would have been returned as a lightbulb"*
>
> Jeroen Carelse, "sarcasm", 2015

Dreaming of a world where you and everyone around you embody unconditional love is a beautiful vision. However, it's essential to remain grounded in reality. Picture yourself swimming among hungry sharks with a bleeding leg—no amount of love can transform the sharks into harmless creatures. This stark image highlights the necessity of discernment.

In this life, your physical body is a finite and irreplaceable vessel, even if Consciousness itself feels vast and enduring. Protecting your body, mind, and spirit isn't merely an option; it's a fundamental responsibility.

Judgement

This means that opening up also makes you more vulnerable when you are in an environment that is abusive or destructive towards you. You need to learn to judge your environment; judgement is good, needed, and useful. Acting poorly on your judgement is something entirely different, and I have noticed painful confusion among people. A blanket statement such as "you shall not judge" or "judging is bad" is a counterproductive thought, which, if followed blindly, leads to self-harm.

You should judge from simple decisions like whether you can cross the street now to more significant ones, like determining if someone is a good person to be with. If you cannot cross the street, there is no need to swear at the cars or act worse. If you find that a certain person does not suit your desires or needs, then there is no need to be antagonistic. Gracefully leave the situation and add the experience to your memory. Time will tell if your judgement was justified.

There are worse-case scenarios, such as being threatened directly or indirectly. Good judgement of the situation helps you decide what to do. Good judgement is certainly aided by knowing yourself, understanding which patterns run you behind the scenes, and recognising your true values. Here authenticity is helpful, as, for example, with my approach, you uncover fears and misguided ideas. These fears and ideas, as written about, especially in the chapter on forces and throughout the book, are not necessarily your fears. As you remove those fears and misguided ideas – also the wishful and positive thinking kind– you are left with who you are.

Authentic judgement surpasses decisions driven by fear, illusion, and delusion.

Authenticity

Authenticity Formula and Practises
I work on improving myself; I make mistakes, but they are less and less frequent than before. For me, the breakthrough has been seeing the link between my improved state of being and being authentic. My definition of authenticity is inspired by a quote from an interview with Gabriel García Márquez:

> "Everyone has three lives: a secret life, a private life, and a public life."
>
> Interview by Gerald Martin
September 1993
Mexico City

When I read this, I had a profound insight: yes, that is precisely what I am looking for. A person is authentic when those three lives become one. But why can it be so difficult to share the secrets we carry with us? Where do these secrets come from, and how do they develop?

What is their function? How can we gradually move them from the secret part of us into the private life we live and into the public sphere?

I began to work in a structured manner on structuring my authenticity theory, and simultaneously testing it on myself, during 2017. At first, the steps were very scary, but over time, I grew more confident that this was a good method for me. As this method seemed to work for me, I wondered if it would work for other people too. Over a period of years, I began to collect more data and test my theories in real life with others. The results were similar: the reality of people changed for the better.

Finally, it is about what concrete results I can achieve that will bring me closer to my true self. In my model, the authentic Self is the perfect Self. We wouldn't be able to reach this blissful state in an earthly life, but we can come closer and nearer. Not only that, we can create a better life for ourselves and the people around us when we do so, even though we have not yet reached the ultimate blissful state.

What is the use of nice stories if they are not based on our shared reality? How do I measure, and what do I look for as evidence that I am developing in the right direction? Later in this chapter, I look at various ways how to measure progress.

The idea of turning my theory into a formula is my sense of humour. I understand how formulas can scare away people, and I also know I like formulas, as I consider them like magic(k) spells that could both lift the veil of reality and obscure reality through codes and confusion. And so, I set out to make my magic(k) spell—a spell to empower you if you can decipher it.

Authenticity

Formula

Variables:
C: Creativity represents the initial idea and inspiration one has.

F: Fear signifies the initial anxiety regarding, for example, potential rejection and embarrassment.

T: Trust indicates the level of confidence in those with whom one shares their work.

R: Reaction reflects the responses received from friends and family.

A: Authenticity measures how true one remains to their initial ideas.

P: Public Acceptance denotes the extent to which a wider audience embraces the work.

Relationships:
C (Creativity): This serves as the starting point, where one begins with initial ideas.

F (Fear): This variable is initially high, representing the fears one faces. However, it tends to diminish over time, as progress is made through various stages.

T (Trust): Trust increases, as one shares their work with individuals they regard as trustworthy.

R (Reaction): Positive feedback from trusted individuals can boost one's confidence.

A (Authenticity): Authenticity increases as confidence grows, allowing one to remain more aligned with their original ideas.

P (Public Acceptance): This is influenced by both the level of authenticity displayed and the overall quality of the work presented.

Formula:
Let's assume Authenticity (**A**) is a function of Creativity (**C**) diminished by Fear (**F**) and boosted by Trust (**T**) and Reaction (**R**):

$$A = C \cdot \left(1 - \frac{F}{F_{max}}\right) + \left(\frac{T}{T_{max}} \cdot R\right)$$

Where:
F_max is the maximum possible fear (a normalising factor).

T_max is the maximum possible trust (a normalising factor).

Public acceptance **P** can then be considered a function of Authenticity (**A**): $P = k \cdot A$

Where:

k is a constant representing the impact of authenticity on public acceptance.

Explanation:

Phase 1 (Secret Life):
F is high, **T** and **R** are zero.
Authenticity $A \approx C \cdot \left(1 - \dfrac{F}{F_{max}}\right)$ (low due to high fear).

Phase 2 (Private Life):
F decreases, as one shares their work with trusted people.

T and **R** become positive values.

Authenticity **A** increases as fear diminishes, and positive reactions boost confidence.

Phase 3 (Public Life):
F is minimal or zero, **T** is maximal and R is high.
Authenticity $A \approx C + \left(\dfrac{T_{max}}{T_{max}} \cdot R\right) = C + R$
(high due to low fear and high trust and reaction).

Public acceptance $P = k \cdot A$ is maximised.

6.2
Tools, Techniques, and Exercises
Do It Yourself and take back control

Building authenticity takes time, intention, and some courage. Time is essential, as it allows for small, steady steps that feel natural and lasting. Seeing growth as a spectrum rather than a matter of "all or nothing" means you can progress with manageable shifts rather than large, sudden changes. This gradual approach helps you to build confidence and to be authentic rather than merely acting in a certain way.

Intention is equally important. As explained earlier, intention is the real engine behind what we do, shaping the quality and meaning of our actions. When you set an honest intention, your actions begin to reflect who you truly are rather than responding out of habit or external pressure. Through these exercises, you'll focus on bringing purpose to your choices, gradually building a more genuine way of being.

Courage is also needed, as authenticity often means letting go of old habits and facing fears of judgement or rejection. This requires understanding the layers of fear that shape our behaviour, as outlined in The Anatomy of Fear. It can be difficult to be true to yourself, and each step requires you to trust that you are enough as you are. These exercises encourage you to take small, manageable steps to express your real thoughts, feelings, and intentions.

The exercises that follow are designed to help you align your emotions, intentions, thoughts, words, and actions with your true values and beliefs. You'll begin by identifying and understanding fears that hold you back, then learn ways to reduce their impact through self-reflection and building trust with others.

Each step offers a practical way to feel more comfortable being your true self, starting with smaller interactions and progressing at your pace. This approach isn't about immediate change, but rather about consistent steps that let you ease into a more open and authentic life.

The exercises will also help you see the positive effects of aligning your emotions, intentions, thoughts, words, and actions—both in how you feel and in how others respond. By tracking your progress, you'll begin to recognise the moments when you feel fully yourself. In time, you may even feel ready to support others on their path to authenticity, sharing your insights with those around you.

Phase 1—it is all in your head: Secret Life

Step 1:Identify Root Fears (Fear Component, *F*)

Task:
Write down your ideas or projects that you hesitate to share. For each, list the specific fears holding you back (e.g., fear of embarrassment, rejection, criticism). Check the 'Anatomy of Fears' for a structural overview of the various kinds of higher-level fears and how they relate to the most primal fears.

Example:
"I like to make an oil painting of nude people"
For years, you wanted to paint nude people. It is unclear to you why, but each time the idea came up you felt this strong drive, immediately overshadowed by fears and doubts.

Examples of thoughts that go on in your head:
"If I make the painting with nude people in it, people might think I'm a sex-obsessed person."
"Why do I fear sharing my creative ideas?"
"What would happen to me?"

> *Fear Mapping: For each identified fear, trace it back to its core concern. Is it a fear of social exclusion, failure, or inadequacy? Keep asking "why" until you uncover a fundamental fear.*
>
> **Imagination:**
> "they think I am a pervert, a sex addict and weird"
>
> "if I share this idea they (friends, family, co-workers, etc.) will always remember it and can never let go of the idea I am a pervert, sex addict or just weird"
>
> "the people around me will reject me"
>
> "they will tell their friends too, and shame me"
>
> "I shall not know who has been told about my idea, and I feel very insecure among even unknown people"
>
> "I will have less and fewer friends and places to go to."

These are thoughts that have a lot to do with the fear of abandonment and isolation

Let's move on to the next step and imagine some possible questions for yourself. That step helps to understand which fears are based on experience and which mind games. There are many more possible variations, but you get an idea of how to get started.

Step 2: Diminish the Fear (Diminishing *F*)

> *Question the basis of each fear. Ask yourself if there is actual evidence to support it or if it's a product of assumptions or experiences. This helps separate realistic concerns from irrational fears.*
>
> **"They think I am a pervert, a sex addict, weird"**
> Have they ever said paintings of nude people are disgusting?
>
> Have they ever said painters who paint nude people are weird, or worse?
>
> But have you ever asked all those people?
>
> Have you seen those all people be very unpleasant towards those artists?
>
> And have they ever expressed discomfort or disapproval when others discuss or create similar artistic themes?

If I share this idea they will always remember it and can never let go of the idea I am a pervert, sex addict or just weird.
Have they ever shown this kind of behaviour?

And have you ever shared something with them that they brought up at inconvenient moments in later times?

Have they ever made negative remarks about others who share similar ideas in the past?

"They reject me" and "They will tell others and shame me"
Have they ever shown this kind of behaviour?

Have they the habit of shaming people, making people feel uncomfortable?

Do they have they a narrow-minded worldview?

I shall not know any more than they have told and feel very insecure among people, as they might know about my idea for a painting
Have they ever shared your personal information without permission before?

Are they the only people you can share this idea with, or show the painting too?

Is there evidence that all these people gossip nastily about friends and people they know?

I will have less and fewer friends and places to go to
Have you experienced similar outcomes after sharing personal ideas in the past?

Do you believe your social circles are limited to what you currently have?

Are all people in your social circle like how you see them above?

As I hope you can see, complexity increases, and the above is only a broad brushstroke of possible mind games that you could play. Some questions you can answer directly, like you know they (friends, family, co-workers) ever shared your deeply personal information without permission.

Worst-case scenario

The above list of fears and worries is strong on "Social and Relational Fears" and "Existential and Identity-Based Fears". You can check with the chapter on "Forces", for example. Take the worst ones you can find and list them below. I chose "Loss of Identity within the Group", "Loss of Social Status or Respect" and "Isolation" but there are quite a few others that would fit in addition.

Now remember, until this point, nothing has happened aside from you playing some mind games. You have not told anyone about your painting idea, nor did you make the painting.

Next you take the fears and order them in the most awful first and least on the bottom:

> *Isolation*
>
> *Loss of Identity within the Group*
>
> *Loss of Social Status or Respect*
>
> **First question: will you physically survive if all of the above would happen?**
> *Assuming you have enough income to survive, and a roof above your head, the answer is yes and we continue. If the answer is no, you have a serious challenge in life and the coming strategy needs careful attention.*
>
> **Second question: will you manage to make new friends?**
> *Assuming you are a relatively social person and have managed so far in life to have a few friends, it is also imaginable you find new ones.*
>
> **Third question: with your true desires in mind, could you imagine finding people who are also interested in fine arts and nude fine arts?**
> *Think of art classes, where people often draw and paint live nudes.*

The logic is: Imagine the worst happens, can you imagine an alternative?

Regardless if you are full of enthusiasm or despair at this point, we are only in the first phase of mapping out the fears and worries. At least you now have a reasonable idea of what could go wrong, that you could find alternatives, and that the fears and worries are only inside your head.

Phase 2: From Secret to Private

Step 3: Building Trust (Trust Component, *T*)

So here we are still wanting to paint nudes and with a basic understanding of what you are actually afraid of. What next?

Would any of your fears become reality if:
You do paint the painting and no one sees it?

You paint the painting, but no one would ever know it is yours.

I find it reasonable to assume the answer to those questions is not.

Thus, you can paint the painting as long as the above conditions apply. You can even paint many paintings like that and keep them secret for the rest of your life, or destroy them after you painted them. Is that a path I advise? No, certainly not. But if your environment is such that you really cannot show who you truly are, then keeping your work secret is a second-best option.

Having a closet full of paintings and no one to admire them is not an artist's dream. You likely would love to share the works too. You know what the worst-case scenarios are, and you know you will recover from those scenarios. But who wants to go through unnecessary misery if it can be avoided?

Here you have quite a few options again, and feel free to be creative and find new ones or combine some. I cannot list them all and wouldn't even know all the options available to you. What I have found is that the Internet gives great opportunities to publish work anonymously, for example. What also works is sharing your idea of painting nudes with a trusted friend. This friend could be someone you occasionally see, but who is open-minded enough to respectfully listen and enquire about your motivations. You only need one such friend, family member, or co-worker, for example.

Share the idea first. Listen to their concerns and encouragement. Ask if the friend would like to follow the progress and see the result. Getting someone involved in the process breaks this exciting journey into smaller periods where you can take in feedback and adjust your strategy. The result, nude people on canvas in oil paint, won't come as a big surprise to your friend any longer. Hence, the chance of a favourable critique is reasonable.

If you decide to take the anonymous Internet route, the same applies. Take people with you on your journey. Write texts that accompany your project and let people give their feedback. There are always people who are themselves in a bad spot in life and react poorly. That is life, and you have to get used to it as a nude oil-painter fine artist.

The result is you make small steps towards a once very scary goal. As your friends or your Internet followers have seen your work, start making more and more.

Some desires are too complex, too controversial, or too big a step for you to realise them in real life. Having these desires, inclinations, or urges is part of being human. I believe you can find a balance between the extremes of executing those urges and repressing them. I suggest that you write a story about your initial thoughts. In it, you can imagine how your character navigates from their initial desires to the wider world consequences.

When you write a story about your desires, you automatically feel which concepts resonate with your truth and which do not. If you find that challenging, go back to the chapter on manifesting and look for the exercise in finding your truth. When I still gave lectures at a university in Helsinki, I taught a class on scenario writing. Scenario writing was only one of the many tools the students were expected to learn, and the lecture was brief, focussing on creating very short scenarios. These scenarios were primarily about testing product and service ideas, but my method applies here too.

Aside from the direct benefits of knowing how to write a scenario, the biggest benefit I realised was that people could overcome their fear of writing a 'fantasy' story. So, I gave the students a rigid framework:

> *Three text blocks of about 50-100 words each:*
> The first block introduces the main character and the challenge one or more characters face.
>
> The second block describes being engaged in the challenge and experiencing the results.
>
> The third block provides a resolution, solution, or conclusion of what happened and perhaps an explanation.

These short stories resulted in fantastic narratives that offered a forward view of possible and often unexpected problems a student had not envisioned yet. Crucial was the attitude and mindset of the student. If the student only wanted to follow the 'rules' and please the teacher (me), then the scenarios were bland, uninspiring, and not very useful to anybody. I think you recognise some fears already there.

Thus, instead of acting on your dark urges, write about them in an enticing, exciting, but authentic way. Then follow the steps outlined in this chapter. You might choose to remain anonymous, depending on the gravity of your literal exploits.

Step 4: Integrate Positive Reaction (Reaction Component, *R*)

One friend's opinion is good; two friends even better. The objective is to lose the fear of "Loss of Identity within the Group", "Loss of Social Status or Respect" and "Isolation". You achieve this by increasing your audience and gaining experience, ensuring you have neither lost your identity within the group, your social status or respect, nor are you isolated. Now that you have this experience, let's grow our group of trusted friends.

Find another friend, family member, co-worker, or another person you can relate to and who shares interests in what you desire to explore in life—in this case, nude painting. Either repeat the process with other people or start asking if they would like to see your new, private hobby. Tell them it is about painting nudes in oil paint, so they are not unpleasantly surprised.

Now, it is a matter of gathering positive and less positive feedback. The more people you show your work to, the more varied the opinions. It may come as no surprise that people comment on the technique, choice of colours, size of the canvas (or panel), and some details in the painting. You might hear, "I like landscape paintings" or "I like Van Gogh". Some comments are helpful; others are merely thoughts that people share with you.

Still, the world did not come to an end. In fact, at this stage, you will start to be more concerned about the technique and choice of colours, and the nude aspect might not even be so exciting any longer. Actively recognise and appreciate the support and enthusiasm of those you trust. This reinforces a positive experience around sharing and may help reduce the internal emphasis on fear.

Phase 3 – From Private to Public

Step 5: Embody Authenticity (Authenticity Component, A)

Evaluate how closely your current work aligns with your true Self and ideas. Ask yourself, "Am I expressing what I genuinely believe and care about?" Adjust if necessary to stay true to your core ideas. Do you feel you have naturally evolved, or have new fears cropped up, such as "Is my technique good enough?" or "Am I not colour-blind?" As you grow and become more authentic, you will experience how past fears dissipate and new ones emerge.

The more you trace high-level fears and worries back to the core issues, like you practised in Phase 1, the easier it becomes. You recognise them from a mile away and might jokingly say, "Oh, there is Mr Rejection again," or "Mrs Unworthiness." You will realise more quickly how most of these fears are leftovers from earlier experiences. Although some might have been deeply hurtful, it is beneficial to check up on them and assess if you still need them. More often than not, you simply don't.

Aside from fears leaving the stage and new ones popping up, the intensity of the fears also begins to wear off. As you make a habit of examining these fears and understanding what they represent, the deeper part of you—the unconscious awareness—learns that most of the fears are not primal fears and there is not much to worry about. As your initial fears have subsided, take a moment to acknowledge this. Take your old list from earlier and read your concerns about what might happen in your life when you paint nude people. Confirm for yourself that either the fears were ungrounded or that you have found a way to circumvent the consequences, for example, by finding new friends.

It is easier to understand the journey towards authenticity when you can see the contrast between the past and present. Before you were worried about losing friends, social status and more. Now you have experienced, you can do what you desire to do, and still flourish in life. However, always check if your desires are supportive to others, and not intentionally cause harm, distress, or worse to other people. You have free will, but you should not interfere with the free will of others.

Step 6: Measure Public Acceptance (Public Acceptance Component, *P*)

Now that you have gained confidence as friends and a relatively small social circle accepts you for who you are, it is time to expand into the wider world. At its core, this step is nothing more or less than once making a public statement and, in your case, showing a nude painting you like most. This can be done in any public venue, online or offline. And then that step is done.

You might feel tempted to spread your wings and show to an increasingly wider audience your achievements, and that is fine. A question you could ask yourself is, why? Why do I feel the need to show the world my paintings? Is this pride talking a form of lust, as the attention is seductive and energising? Chapter 3 "Cardinal Sins and Virtues" shows a framework that helps you to navigate these temptations. Furthermore, these temptations, when getting closer to their extreme endpoints, can be understood as either expressions of fears or external influences that take hold of you.

And so for each step of growing your authentic self, challenges arise. And this is a good sign; a change in challenges very well could show how old patterns and habits have begun to shift. The more people you now reach, the more varied and perhaps intense the feedback will be. This is normal and there shall be people who deeply despise what you do, and people who truly love all your work. Use feedback as a tool for growth, refine your next project to enhance your authenticity. By treating feedback as information rather than validation, you can continuously improve your authentic self-expression and not fall victim to pride and indulgence.

By following these steps, you can apply the "Authenticity formula" in a structured way, gaining insight into how diminishing fear and increasing trust contribute to more authentic self-expression. The example I gave was from my life, slightly modified only. I hope you could resonate with it.

You can try any desire-fear situation, such as changing professions, moving to another country and making changes in your relationship. The formula also works for minor decisions, such as eating a piece of gorgeous cake without you fearing this damages your health, smoking this special cigar at a party and not fearing getting ill. Or you finally want to make the study of astrology an important part of your life and not hide that you find it a fascinating topic, worth exploring further.

6.3
Recognising progress
Progress, Stagnation, or Decline

After my earlier realisation that programmes and obsolete strategies were influencing parts of my decision-making process, I began piecing together bits of information, anecdotes, and personal experiences. I discovered nuggets of insight in many disciplines, but the theory that resonated most with me was Tom's idea about the LCS. I say it resonated because I could listen, absorb, and reflect without feeling resistance. Likewise, I wouldn't believe everything he said, but there was a calmness in me that could be phrased as, "Okay, sounds interesting, let's see about that."

Tom's attitude of encouraging anyone to test his findings and his reference to "the proof of the pudding is in the eating" gave me a further sense of having found a solid foundation. Still, the sceptical side of me wanted evidence, proof, and intellectual certainty. The emotional and intuitive part felt at ease. I had an enormous sense of urgency to fix my life; I had to follow his advice and test, test, and test. In an email exchange with Tom, he answered my question, "But how do I know I am making progress?" with a simple answer: "Look at the people around you, how they react to you. That will tell you in which direction you are evolving." Well, I can immediately see that, although making, for example, a distinction between being a pleaser, a doormat, or conforming could also make others around me "happy" but me unhappy.

Thus, I needed to be not only observant of others, but also certain of what was happening deep inside me. I had to ensure I would not fall back into some old survival patterns and instead learn to be myself. What does this "being myself" mean? I know that when I feel great, successes begin to unfold in my life and when I feel lousy, life is filled with failures. So, how can I create that in a more consistent manner?

Being who I am, I considered how to measure my progress. The basic idea of measurement involves comparing situation A to situation B, location A to location B, time A to time B, and so forth. To measure progress in the quality of your life, as I define authenticity, you can identify how you feel and how others feel about you.

Thus, how do you feel before an interaction with someone, and how do you feel afterward? How do you feel about interacting with this person now compared to a while ago? How do you feel about discussing certain topics with this person before and after? And how does this person react to you in those situations? The variations of before and after are seemingly endless, and you can begin testing at any moment, even by reflecting on your experiences.

The previous chapters have given you various insights into understanding and interacting with this reality, the forces at play, and discovering who you are through your true desires, to name a few. Next I offer ideas and strategies to measure where you have been, where you are now and where you will be in the future, helping you see if progress has been made in any direction, form, or shape.

In the next section, I look at three dimensions you can use to gauge progress:

you vs the other
happy vs unhappy
success vs failure

Your growth is a unique, evolving journey—one that doesn't fit into a one-size-fits-all mould. To better understand where you've been, where you are now, and where you're heading, measuring personal growth can offer valuable insights. However, it's important to remember that these measurements should be flexible, self-paced, and empowering, not burdensome or restrictive.

At its core, measuring personal growth is about identifying patterns and trends in your life. It allows you to notice shifts in your reactions, habits, and mindset, providing a clearer picture of your progress over time. Whether it's observing your emotional responses, evaluating how you handle challenges, or assessing your approach to goals, each measurement offers a reflection of your journey.

> *Personal growth can be quantified through delta-T (ΔT), a measure of change over a specific period.*

The key to meaningful measurement is developing your own system. While common methods like journalling, self-reflection, or tracking habits can be helpful, the most significant thing is creating a system that feels right for you. This process isn't about following rules or sticking to strict timelines; it's about finding a way to observe your growth that feels personal and empowering. Perhaps you measure growth through moments of self-awareness or by tracking how your mindset shifts after tough situations. The possibilities are endless, and the choice is yours.

The benefits of measuring personal growth are significant. It can increase your self-awareness, helping you identify areas of strength and opportunity. It can also serve as motivation, reminding you of how far you've come and reinforcing your commitment to continue evolving. Most importantly, it creates a sense of self-empowerment. By creating your own system, you take ownership of your growth process.

Remember, personal growth is not a race, and there's no finish line. Your journey will evolve, and so will the ways you measure it. Whether you track progress occasionally or use your system on a whim, the most important thing is that you feel empowered to measure growth in a way that suits you. Trust in the process and in yourself—personal growth is an ongoing journey, not a destination.

I provide examples of how astrology can function as a map to give direction and to measure progress. Additionally, astrology can help you identify more and less optimal moments to start specific activities. Next, I illustrate how dreams, fantasies, and premonitions reveal your current position in life, the desires you may hold, and the fears that actively influence you. "Letter to my Future Self" is another way to measure your progress, as you compare your desires for your future with what you have achieved.

Many people have been in various relationships—intimate ones, business partnerships, and more casual friendships. Looking back on some of these relationships, you can see how you could have handled situations better. In other situations, it's easier to blame the other person. In cases like abusive relationships, you should have left much earlier and not given in to fears of abandonment. With experience, you have the chance to grow. You need a wide variety of experiences to learn who you are and what you want.

Later in life, you may see the problems in these relationships much more clearly and much earlier, but still ignore many of the tell-tale signs that things are wrong. The feedback you receive from being in the experience and doing the exercise is your data point, your measure moment. Consider an abusive relationship—not too extreme, but annoying enough that you feel drained after a conversation because the other person talks aggressively back at you when you disagree. You can still see some good sides of them, making it challenging to decide to end the relationship.

Among the various choices you have is to leave, to tolerate all the ignoring and subtle insults, to start doing the same and become verbally aggressive, or explore a few more options. One option is to use this relationship to build strength, grow, and contribute to becoming more authentic. See it as going to the gym; you are standing there and see all the weights lying on the floor. You can kick at the weights, shout at them, and get upset. Or you can start with the weight you can handle well, practice, and when the time is right, move on to a heavier weight until you reach your goal.

The same approach applies to relationships. You could continue the conversation while adjusting how often you interact with the other person. Perhaps the frequency of talking was too high, so now you manage the pacing or the number of interactions more thoughtfully. You might respond neutrally when a sensitive topic arises—not necessarily agreeing, but stopping at a phrase like, "That's interesting," or another expression that holds minimal weight. Alternatively, you could try asking a question instead of offering a statement. Various strategies exist to navigate these social obstacles, each requiring experimentation and a sense of what works and what doesn't.

Feedback comes to us many times a day—in our waking state, our dream state, and the moments in between. This constant flow of feedback offers us repeated opportunities to listen and sense where we stand in our growth. The LCS has all kinds of environments and experiences, including dreams, fantasies, and meditative states, that function differently from our waking physical reality. Within these states, individuals can access insights into aspects of themselves that are often less accessible in daily life.

Astrology

My interest in astrology began as a teenager, reading horoscopes in magazines. I noticed, however, that even signs apart from my could also feel relevant to me. I kept looking at the magazine horoscopes and, through the ideas I absorbed as a child, became fascinated with planets and stars, exploring how celestial bodies influence their surroundings. Reading about the influence of the sun and moon on natural patterns on planet Earth, I began to wonder if human emotions and behaviours could also be affected by these forces—an idea that has stayed with me over the years.

In my late thirties, I came across the work of Raymond Dewey on natural cycles, which provided me with new insights into cosmic influences. My exploration of astrology itself, however, remained limited until I began reflecting on my behavioural patterns. Recalling a natal chart reading from my teenage years, I noticed that some descriptions of my future identified back then had actualised later in adulthood, which reawakened my interest in astrology.

My first reading

This must have been in the early 80s, and one day I went home after school with a female friend of mine. They had a guest, an older lady, and she and I began to chat. At some moment, she asked if she could 'do my natal chart,' to which I positively reacted. She could read from that chart things about my health, like sensitivity to certain herbs, some pivotal moments around the age of 8—which I still have not figured out—and a few more things related to the past or current time.

There were many more intriguing topics, such as how specific shapes (squares and trines or triangles) are supposed to convey a fundamental message. They symbolise a strong determination to create or be creative, as well as a focus on reasoning and logic. Similar descriptions I took as flattering, and some as warning signs—traits that I would rather not have. But what lost me was when she began to talk more about my future.

I was supposed to move to a Scandinavian or Nordic country in my early twenties. When I was there, I began to start teaching, having teaching jobs. Now, one of the things I deeply despised at that age was school, teachers, and the whole idea of education in the traditional way. After being initially impressed with the accuracy, I felt let down by the "teacher" forecast, and I barely listened to the rest of her analysis.

Suffice it to say, I moved to Finland in my early twenties, started teaching, and later became a lecturer at a university and polytechnics.

The entire idea of astrology as somewhat beneficial did stick with me, and I took the advice to remove mint from my 'diet'. I can't say if there is direct causation, but after I switched toothpaste and stopped chewing on chewing gum or ate candies with mint, my breathing got a lot easier. I do not mind experimenting and failures I care little about. Through experimentation and accepting failure, I learn fast. People around me might see this as me trying things and not finishing what I started, but that is not how this feels to me at all.

Reflecting on Tarot

> For my 50th birthday, a friend gave me a beautiful tarot deck, the Golden Visconti Tarot. The cards are richly decorated with gold accents and intricate illustrations, which I have admired for years without really knowing how to use them. Eventually, I decided to make them part of my daily routine. Since I would rather not study tarot in depth among my other interests, I created a simple system.

> Each morning, I shuffle the deck, pick three cards at random, and set them on my desk. I use specific meanings I found online, based on Jungian archetypes, to interpret each card. At first, I thought these daily draws might predict what would happen, but I soon realised the cards, in the way I used them, worked differently. Rather than revealing events, they pointed to three qualities or themes that I could observe throughout the day.

> This daily practice showed me how symbolic tools can help focus awareness on specific aspects of life. The three cards provide traits or patterns to watch for, which often show up in me or in situations around me. This approach doesn't foretell the future but helps prompt attention to certain themes or behaviours. Each combination of cards brings different ideas to mind, which I recognise in my experiences as the day unfolds.

Gradually, this approach with the tarot cards helped me see how other symbolic systems, like astrology, might offer similar insights. Perhaps astrology is more like a map that shows potentiality?

I came to see astrology as a guide to our inherent qualities tendencies and challenges—a kind of "map" we each carry from birth, visible in an astrological chart. Whether the positions of celestial bodies at birth influence the human Soul directly, or serve simply as markers indicating specific traits and potential life events, astrology offers a way to understand oneself and to time one's decisions. Historically, astrology allowed ancient cultures, including the Babylonians and Egyptians, to connect human life with cosmic cycles.

Astrology can be a flexible guide for self-understanding. A natal chart reveals personality traits and potential challenges. Although it does not predict exact outcomes, astrology can enhance self-awareness, assist in relationships, and identify favourable times for decisions. Many people view astrology as either mere superstition or a strict set of predictions. However, a balanced view of astrology states that it indicates when certain tendencies or outcomes may be more likely. This shows that while certain outcomes are more likely than others, knowing these tendencies through your natal chart helps you recognise them in real life. This recognition can, over time, reinforce the relevance of the chart, allowing it to serve as a valuable tool for deeper self-understanding.

I consider astrology as a way to observe life's rhythms through a sort of cosmic clock, where celestial bodies act as markers indicating possible influence. While the effects of the sun and moon on Earth are well understood, other celestial bodies might exert subtler forces. By using astrology as a tool for self-discovery and timing, you can approach life with greater intention, using insights to guide you rather than limit your choices based on routines, habits, and ingrained patterns.

A Blueprint of Potentials and Qualities

Astrology offers a detailed framework for understanding human personality and potential. The positions of planets in zodiac signs and houses reveal specific characteristics and influences that shape individuals. Each placement adds to the intricate nature of personal traits and tendencies, providing insights into how these factors interact to influence one's identity and life experiences.

To illustrate, one remark I hear from people is something like "I am a Virgo and I know people who are a Virgo, but they are not like me at all". Curious about these matters as I am, I did some experimentation with variability. The sun sign, what people often refer to as "horoscope signs," is only one aspect of a much more intricate narrative. Consider how the Sun's position in different signs and houses reveals various facets of a person's personality. While interpretations of placements and rulerships can vary widely among astrologers, I hope the examples below help to show that there is more depth to astrology than the simple statement, "I'm a Virgo."

Here are some examples involving the Sun Virgo:

Sun in Virgo in the 1st House:
Those with the Sun in Virgo in the 1st house frequently present themselves as practical and detail-oriented. They typically possess a strong sense of duty and may project a reserved or analytical demeanour, placing significant importance on efficiency and organisation.

Sun in Virgo in the 2nd House:
This placement may lead to a marked focus on work ethic and resource management. Such individuals typically find self-worth in their skills and contributions, frequently pursuing careers in service-oriented fields, healthcare, or analysis.

Sun in Virgo in the 3rd House:
With the Sun in Virgo in the 3rd house, individuals tend to excel in communication and the gathering of information. They usually enjoy acquiring and sharing knowledge, displaying a sharp, analytical mind that seeks clarity and precision in discussions.

These examples show how the same zodiac signs—such as Virgo—can manifest uniquely depending on their house placement, emphasising the interaction between a sign's traits and the influences of each house. While interpretations of these placements may vary, the key takeaway is that a simplistic view of astrology is limiting and leads to misguided criticism.

To further highlight this complexity, consider the total mathematical possibilities of planetary placements in astrology. There are 137 billion (137,858,491,849) possible configurations when only accounting for 10 celestial bodies—the Sun, Moon, and eight planets—positioned across 12 houses. Other significant astrological factors, such as Chiron, the North and South Nodes, and additional variables, can further increase the number of variations. This impressive figure demonstrates the broad range of potential combinations that can exist in a natal chart.

However, not all of these combinations are realistic in astrological practice. The arrangement of planets in a natal chart typically reflects common configurations observed in typical cases. By estimating that approximately 30% of the total placements are plausible, we arrive at around 41 billion (41,357,547,555 realistic configurations).

These configurations allow for the natural distribution of planets, including shared house placements (such as a stellium) and the presence of empty houses. This exploration of variations underscores that while the number of possible configurations is vast, the individual placements of a planet in a specific sign and household considerable significance. Each unique combination can reflect distinct features in a person's character, motivations, and life experiences. Astrology not only offers numerous possibilities, but also helps us understand how these possibilities interact to shape our lives.

The Role of Astrology in Self-Discovery
Imagine that the idea of the positions of planets, the sun, and the moon and related bodies is like a map for your potential and purposes in life. This means that you can use this map to measure your current state and compare that with your intended state. Let say an astrological analysis suggests in this phase of your life you are, or should be, engaged in exploring the world. Now you wonder about this, as you are not much of a traveller. Is this suggestion of exploring the world wrong, or should you understand "travelling" through a different lens? Is this about the physical world, a mental world, or perhaps even a spiritual world?

Even though various interpretations are possible, you get an idea to reflect on and use as a data point to think more about. Moreover, explore in your mind how you feel about the other kinds of "exploring the world". Do you feel resistance or anxiety when you think of travelling to another country? Chapter 6 on Authenticity gives you guidelines on how to explore those and deal with them.

Aside from a possible purpose at a given period in your life, the astrological analysis is also useful to see where some potential is stronger or weaker. Thus, certain phases of your life get a little push from the LCS to get stuff done. This is how I describe it to myself, and now share this blunt analogy with you. In my sceptical moments, I look at such an analysis like I consider the tarot-card experiment. There is an aspect of a kind of self-fulfilling prophecy, which I find practical and useful. And if this works, why not use it?

Synastry: you and the other
Astrology can play a role in understanding relationship dynamics. Different types of relationships contribute to both positive and negative growth. Harmonious relationships nurture support and encouragement, while challenging relationships offer opportunities for deep personal insights and transformation. In most cases, an intimate relationship is a mix of all kinds of challenges and opportunities. Astrological compatibility can provide insights into potential conflicts and strengths within relationships, though this exploration will not be in-depth. But is it that straightforward?

Since developing a more profound interest in astrology, I have begun to explore its various interpretations, purposes, and techniques. I am only starting to learn about the techniques and calculations, but the purposes and interpretations have become more familiar to me. One intriguing purpose is examining relationships through the lens of astrology. I did so several times, but each time I was disappointed, as my spouse and I appeared to have one of the worst possible combinations, if not the worst. Only recently did I gain an insight that changed my interpretations.

> *We have had our ups and downs, some quite intense, but after almost three decades together, we are doing very fine. Of course, this doesn't align with what astrology suggests. The worst possible relationship horoscope, synastry, and yet we're doing fine—how can that be explained? I didn't like the idea of turning a negative into a positive by mental gymnastics. However, when I took a step back and considered the concepts of purpose, life's lessons, growth, and authenticity—the weights in the gym—a new picture began to form.*

> *This relationship presented some rather interesting and intense challenges. By this point, I had learned to look through various lenses, stepping back to fundamentally consider life as a controlled chain*

reaction of experiences. To open up my thinking, I applied my favourite tool: think 180 degrees. Think the opposite and see what appears before you. So, what if this 'worst possible result' was, in fact, the best thing that could happen to me?

What if these hard lessons are beneficial? I pondered. I consider myself a keen explorer and learner, and as my Mercury placements suggest, "not too stupid" either. Not only that, but I'm not only driven by a sense of urgency, I also have a desire to make up for missed opportunities and potentially lost time. So, what if this relationship actually aids me in accelerated growth?

Plenty of books are written about astrology and related topics such as astrotheology. I have merely started to scratch the surface of this, for me, a fascinating subject. There is so much more to consider and explore. I leave this section with some of the aspects that might inspire you.

Timing, Context, and Free Will in Astrology
Timing and context are pivotal in astrology, particularly concerning significant life events. Astrological transits can deeply influence personal decisions and experiences, underscoring the importance of being aware of these celestial movements. However, astrology is inherently non-deterministic, providing valuable insights while respecting personal choice and free will. It harmoniously coexists with other belief systems centred on agency, offering guidance without enforcing strict predestination.

Astrology's Role in Navigating External Influences and Personal Growth
Beyond personal decision-making, astrology aids in managing external challenges, including influences from malevolent non-human intelligence (NHI). Understanding planetary positions and houses empowers individuals to comprehend how these factors impact their abilities and choices. Utilising astrological techniques can serve as protective measures, enabling informed decisions amidst external pressures. Additionally, astrology is a powerful tool for personal growth and self-awareness, helping individuals identify their

strengths and weaknesses, set meaningful goals, and nurture self-development. It remains one of many resources available for those seeking deeper self-discovery and improvement.

Dreams

In the dream state, the usual limitations of waking life no longer apply. Dreams seem to follow a different set of rules. For example, movement can feel unnatural, as if you're trying to run, but your legs are heavy, almost like wading through water.

This experience of "wading through water" can sometimes reflect how we feel in waking life. In some situations, we may feel similar resistance when trying to make progress, even with strong effort. For example, a person may feel stuck in an unfulfilling routine or held back by self-doubt when pursuing a new goal. Just as the water in the dream gives a feeling "stuck-ness".

Or "wading through water" has an entirely different meaning. There are many schools of thought on this topic. I am by no means a learned person when it comes to dream interpretation in general. In my dreams I have begun to get more and more after careful reflection.

> *It was only some months before I began with my first draught of this book, in 2018 perhaps, that I began to read a page here and there on Carl Jung. I had heard of him and had some very general idea of the kinds of thoughts he had about dreams and psychology in general. I have not yet read much by him nor Marie Louise von Franz, but what I have read and heard regarding dreams and its relevance I subscribe to.*

Time in dreams often feels flexible and unpredictable. You may find yourself in one place one moment, and in an entirely different place the next. Your perspective may also change, shifting from seeing things through your eyes to observing yourself from a distance. These shifts add to the fluid nature of dreams.

As you grow in your waking lives and begin to live more authentically, you may also notice changes in your influence within the dream state. Obstacles in dreams, such as the feeling of wading through water, may start to feel less restrictive. For instance, after a strong realisation in waking life, you may find yourself moving freely in dreams, discovering that barriers that once seemed solid can now be bypassed with intent.

This reflects how, in waking life, obstacles that once felt like barriers are now considered opportunities for growth (as discussed in the chapter on Forces) and no longer have to hold you back. Your approach to obstacles—or, instead, to passages or opportunities—may also shift, shaping how you view both waking reality and your experiences in dreams. In turn, this change in perspective can affect the dream state, where experiences that once felt negative or challenging may now seem neutral or even positive.

Dreams often feel like being at the mercy of outside forces, as though you're a pinball in a machine. You are carried along, with limited power to interact or shape the outcome. Yet, as you grow, the experience of being in dreams changes; personal growth can bring a greater sense of control, while also shifting the overall nature of the dream itself.

Living more authentically in waking life does not mean total control in dreams—nor is that needed. Rather, the themes of dreams become less chaotic and intense, reducing the sense of needing to control the experience. And when you experience control in a dream, you do not necessarily consider it to be a bad thing. Your perception of "something bad" in a dream gradually shifts into "an obstacle" or "something to overcome".

A form of dreaming called Lucid Dreaming is more or less an in-between state of being consciously aware and dreaming. Whereas you in (sleep) dreams you feel the "stuck-ness" of walking through water, in a lucid dream you can now learn to fly over the water, or reach the destination in a blink of an eye. This requires practice and patience, and you might find this interesting to explore on your own.

For me, dreams act as a mirror, reflecting personal growth and providing insight into my inner life and its main themes. With this in mind, I choose not to try to control my dreams, but instead to observe and learn from them as they unfold. Dreams give me a perspective on the shifts within myself and on the directions in which I am growing.

When I was young, I often had intense nightmares about strange creatures entering my room and taking me away. Later, I realised these types of dreams were fairly common, and they stopped in my early teens. For a long time, I had no nightmares at all. Even the typical dreams where monsters chased me did not appear during these years. This peaceful period continued until I entered a serious relationship. At that point, the nightmares returned, and occasionally, I would even find myself lucid, aware that I was in a nightmare. Most of these dreams seemed to reflect my state of mind at that time, showing up more regularly when I was stressed or anxious.

Over time, though, I began to experience a different kind of nightmare. These dreams were simpler, typically involving me trying to escape but being unable to move fast enough. The threat was something I couldn't see, and I would wake up just as it reached me. Other dreams showed a visible threat, but I had no way of defending myself. As I began focussing on self-reflection and my authenticity exercises, and got a more profound understanding of the principles behind Simulation Theory, I noticed a shift in these dreams. At first, I would find myself holding a weapon in the dream, but my attempts to use it had no effect on whatever was threatening me. Gradually, I developed the ability to stay more present in my dreams, switching between feeling like I was watching and actively participating.

As my level of awareness in these dreams grew, I found that my efforts to defend myself became more effective. This change mirrored a shift I was experiencing in my waking life. I moved away from feeling like a victim in certain areas and started to feel more in control, where seeing myself as a victim no longer made sense. Nightmares have since become rare, and when they do occur, I interpret them as signals about my mental state or some signal that something is not right in my body. They act as road signs, sometimes highlighting unresolved stress and other times marking the progress I am making in my personal development.

Fantasies

Fantasies are imagined scenarios that allow you to mentally engage in experiences beyond what is possible or acceptable in daily life. In these imagined situations, you can try on different versions of yourself, picturing possibilities that don't fit the limits of reality or social expectations. Fantasies might centre on grand success, power, or influence, reflecting hidden desires, insecurities, or hopes. You may experience darker fantasies, which can bring to light fears, anger, or unresolved conflicts that are often kept out of sight.

Rather than you directly act in these imagined situations, thinking about them in a detached way can reveal parts of yourself that are otherwise difficult to address openly, such as difficult emotions or impulsive urges. Fantasies offer a safe mental space for confronting these private aspects of the mind. Typically, reflecting on fantasies through creative outlets like art, writing, or other forms of expression helps you to understand complex emotions and unmet needs.

Interestingly, fantasies may also have a deeper, less obvious role within the LCS. One might consider the idea that certain fantasies connect to unresolved themes or tasks chosen at the beginning of this life, possibly linked to experiences from past lives. These recurring fantasies could act as subtle signals, reflecting areas of growth or challenges the individual has set for themselves across lifetimes. By engaging thoughtfully with these fantasies, you may uncover recurring patterns or underlying themes that hint at personal goals stretching beyond a single lifetime.

In my approach, a gradual process can make it easier to integrate these hidden parts of ourselves (outlined in the chapter Authenticity). This process involves moving your fantasies in stages, from "secret" life to "public" life. At first, your most deeply personal, often darker fantasies are kept hidden deep in your mind, where they can build up tension or emerge unexpectedly as bursts of strong emotion. You move these fantasies from your inner "secret" space into the "private" sphere. In this first step, you begin sharing them with trusted family, friends, or even an anonymous wider audience.

Be aware that you should avoid groups that encourage you to act out harmful fantasies in real life. With responsible sharing, these thoughts can become less intense and any shame or discomfort they cause may go away.

Finally, these previously hidden aspects can be brought into "public" life. At this stage, these fantasies are no longer sources of discomfort but are integrated into one's self-identity. Through this gradual shift—from secret, to private, to public—the meaning of the fantasy often changes, turning a once dark or hidden scenario into a story of self-reflection and growth. In this way, carefully engaging with fantasies not only helps reduce shame and offers a clearer understanding of one's deeper Self, but may also serve as a guide towards fulfilling life tasks within the LCS framework.

Letter to Your Future Self

Writing a Letter to Your Future Self is an introspective activity where you compose a message to yourself, intended for reading at some point in the future. It's a way to capture your current thoughts, feelings, ambitions, and aspirations, serving as a sort of mental time capsule. I also think this method relates to regret and manifestation. By writing down your ambitions with the knowledge that you will read them again, there is a sense of pressure to follow through. Because, if you did not, you would feel bad about yourself for not standing up for yourself. So, once you reach the point where you read the letter and realise that you haven't followed through, you may feel regret over wasted time. However, this regret can motivate you to improve in the future. I would also feel shame if I had not reached my goals, being a sloth, lazy, and a coward perhaps. Here is where the duality of the Seven Sins and Virtues and Fears comes in handy for me. The idea of being a sloth would push me to take action and overrule the fear of, for example, ridicule, or fear of failing.

I have here one way of getting going:

> ***Choose a timeframe:***
> *Determine when you will open the letter—six months, a year, or even five years from now.*
>
> ***Reflect:***
> *Write about your current life, aspirations, challenges, and advice that you want to remember.*

Be honest:
Write down your hopes, fears, and encouragement for yourself.

Store it:
Keep it somewhere safe, or use an online service to send it to yourself at a later date. You can also put the text as a note into a calendar and activate a reminder for that future date.

Benefits:
Self-reflection: helps clarify your priorities and track personal growth.

Goal setting: reinforces your goals, serving as a reminder of your aspirations.

Emotional Support: Offers future encouragement and perspective during tough times.

Let's look back in time

If you can do this for a future moment, imagine you are already now at this future moment. Why not look back at the past six months, one year, or even five years and make a list of the things you wanted to do, you should have done, and make up the balance?

Create a grading system like numbers 1, 2 and 3. Number 1 you use for the least important failures, number 3 for the most important failures, and number 2 sits somewhere in the middle. The importance here is the extra cognitive step you make when you begin to apply these numbers. As you decide whether a missed opportunity holds little importance, slight importance, or great importance, you go on to consider, among other things:

- *Time used or wasted*
- *Opportunities you had and did not take*
- *Past and current emotions*
- *How your life could have been, if...*
- *How relations with others are affected*

You can use these eventual feelings of regret, disappointment, and sadness. These powerful emotions you can turn into sources of determination, focus, and energy. You can see – measure – how time (your chosen timeframe) slips away. Now, this measurement can help you to clarify your next goals.

You can also expand on this exercise. Look at your list and identify certain activities that are particularly hard for you to take action on. Perhaps everything involving other people receives a grade of 3? Think about the chapter on Forces, and consider what fears hold you back, and what other forces push and pull you in different directions.

Looking back on life

> *The first time I read about a person having regrets about certain aspects of his life was in a memoir of a former car manufacturer CEO. In the memoir he retells a situation at the Christmas dinner table where his children were present. In that story, he remarked how much he liked it everybody being present. His family was all here to celebrate Christmas. One of his children remarked something similar to how late it is for him, the father, to appreciate this, as he has been absent his whole life.*

In my early teenage years, I made a resolute decision: I would become a father at a young age. This choice wasn't born out of recklessness but stemmed from a deep desire to offer my children what I had lacked growing up—a father who had time to play. My father, though present in many ways, never took time to play with me, nor my brothers. He was a good father in other ways.

When my first child was born, life had other plans. Circumstances beyond my control robbed me of the opportunity to be the engaged and playful father I had imagined. That lost opportunity left a quiet, deep wound that profoundly shaped how I approached fatherhood later.

With the children who came after, I made a choice: I stayed at home. It felt natural—the fulfilment of the promise I had made to my younger self. Being present wasn't just about physical proximity; it was about being involved, about being true to myself. I became the father I had once longed for. I'm not perfect as a father; I have made my errors, but I try to correct those and explain to my children why I behaved in certain ways. While I couldn't rewrite the past, I found great satisfaction in the moments I shared with my children.

The reading of the memoir and my experiences as a young father had made me consciously aware of the consequences of my choices. And as with much in life, the consequences only show up much later, a long feedback loop so to speak. This desire to be a young and engaged father has served as a form of manifestation and a letter to my future self. Manifesting as I repeated my intentions and imagined me playing with young human beings and having fun. Letter to my future self, as, although I did not send a real letter, I engraved my deepest desires into my memory, which I could recall whenever I wanted to. Like opening the letter and read it.

Hospice experiences

As you might have picked up from this book, I try to find a silver lining in situations that seem dire. You must also have gathered that I don't view death as my endpoint, but rather as a moment for reflection, occurring after the moment of passing. Not surprisingly, many people also look back upon their lives before they move on. I learned to look back often and correct my course. Although feelings of regret and shame have some positives, I would rather not leave this life with those. Instead, I want to face death like William Blake:

> *Just before he died his countenance became fair, his eyes brightened, and he burst out into singing of the things he saw in heaven. In truth, he died like a saint, as a person who was standing by him observed.*
>
> The Life of William Blake,
by Alexander Gilchrist, p. 382

William Blake and Jacob Böhme inspire me. They both wrote about their ideas of reality and tried to visually explain what they envisioned. I read in their works about the fulfilment of living an authentic life. They measure success by this authentic way of living, not by chasing fame, fortune, and trinkets. But you do not have to express yourself as much as Böhme and Blake did to live a satisfying life. Authenticity is not about achievements, but rather being true to one's self, or Soul. Still, life gets complicated, and in hindsight, we could have done certain things, but never did.

Hospices can give good insight into what these regrets – if we can call them that – are. Of course, we talk in general terms and from an industrialised Western perspective as well. What I have gathered are the following common regrets.

Physical and Health-Related Regrets:
Failing to appreciate a healthy body while it was still working properly.

Taking basic physical functions—such as walking, tasting food, or being physically independent—for granted.

Work-Life Balance Regrets:
Prioritising work over family time, friendships and such.

Saying to yourself, you will start to enjoy life after you retire.

Wishing they had taken more time off to enjoy life and embrace the present moment.

Relationship Regrets:
Neglecting to fix or reconcile relationships sooner.

Spending insufficient time with family, friends, or children.

Missing the chance to reconnect with people, assuming there would always be another day.

Authenticity Regrets:
Living according to others' expectations rather than following one's own path.

Overly concerning themselves with others' opinions.

Trying to fit in, or not stand out.

Maintaining a specific image.

Continuing to make choices as if parents were still around.

Avoiding early reflection on potential regrets, delaying opportunities for personal growth and change.

Acting sooner on desires.

Other Regrets:
Regretting decisions or indecision that could have brought greater joy.

Failing to appreciate the simple joys of everyday life.

Select from the list above the three items that you have done well, and three where you failed. Or take them all and make two or three lists: done that well, can be better, and I am not good at either. Check what emotions arise, what thoughts and reasoning you come up with not to take action. All these items from the list and the emotions, thoughts and reasoning you attach to them say something about where you stand now in life. This is a good moment to introduce changes, and check back in a week, a month, or a year from now. Have items from the "am not good at either" list moved to the "can be better" list? Have items from the "can be better" list moved to the "have done well" list? That would indicate progress, congratulations.

NDE stories

Near-death experiences (NDEs), in my opinion, are a fascinating phenomenon because they offer insights into what might happen after death. The International Association for Near-Death Studies (IANDS) has published numerous studies in their Journal of Near-Death Studies exploring these experiences. A single account of an NDE can be intriguing, but hundreds of such stories are even more intriguing. When you read or listen to thousands of accounts, you might begin to wonder if there is something significant to them.

What makes this topic especially relevant for this book and the concept of measuring progress is the commonalities found in these stories. Many accounts describe life after death and the experience of returning to life. A recurring theme is the "life review"—a moment where past actions are revisited and experienced, often from the perspective of those affected by them. This review is frequently described as non-judgmental, serving instead as a reflective opportunity to understand why certain actions were taken and their impact on others.

I find Near-death experiences (NDEs) one of the most fascinating, and potentially, most insightful phenomena. These deeply personal experiences, often occurring during life-threatening situations, and they seem remarkably similar across diverse cultures and backgrounds.

For example, Dr. Bruce Greyson and others show that several common elements emerge from the accounts of those who have undergone NDEs. One of the most frequently reported aspects is the out-of-body experience (OBE), described by approximately 80-90% of NDErs.

This sensation of detachment from the physical body is often accompanied by a profound sense of peace and well-being, reported by about 75-80% of individuals. Many describe feeling free from pain and earthly concerns during this state.

A common feature in approximately 65-70% of near-death experiences (NDEs) is the encounter with a bright, warm light. This light is frequently described as intensely radiant, but not painful to view or experience. Many individuals report feeling drawn to this warm, bright light and perceive it as a source of unconditional love and acceptance.

Around 60-65% of NDErs report meeting deceased relatives, spiritual beings, or religious figures during their experience. These encounters are frequently described as joyful reunions or comforting presences that guide the individual through their journey. This element often coincides with a sense of entering another realm or dimension, reported by approximately 50-60% of NDErs.

Another common feature is altered time perception, experienced by about 60% of individuals. Many describe time as fluid or nonexistent, with past, present, and sometimes future events appearing to occur simultaneously or in rapid succession.

A significant portion of NDErs, around 30-40%, report experiencing a life review. This panoramic replay of one's life events is often described as instantaneous yet comprehensive, allowing the individual to re-experience their actions and understand their impact on others from a new perspective.

This review is frequently accompanied by a sense of cosmic unity or oneness, also reported by about 30-40% of NDErs.

The "tunnel experience" is another well-known aspect of NDEs, described by approximately 30-35% of individuals. This often involves a sense of moving through a dark passageway towards the bright light mentioned earlier.

Similarly, about 30-35% of NDErs describe encountering a boundary or limit, often interpreted as a point of no return.

While less common, some NDErs (around 10-15%) report having precognitive visions during their experience. These may include glimpses of future events or a sudden influx of knowledge about the universe. This aspect of NDEs is particularly intriguing and has been the subject of focused research. Precognitive visions can take various forms:

> *Personal Flash-forwards: Visions of events that will involve the individual personally after their NDE.*
>
> *Global or Prophetic Visions: Previews of planetary-wide events, including both challenging times and periods of spiritual enlightenment.*

> *Expanded Knowledge:* A sudden understanding of the universe's workings and one's place within it, often described as profound and beyond previous comprehension.
>
> *Specific Future Events:* Visions of particular events, ranging from personal milestones to global occurrences, that later come to pass.
>
> *Altered Perception of Time:* A sense that the past, present, and future exist simultaneously, losing their linear quality.

It's worth noting that not all NDEs include every feature, and the sequence of events can vary significantly between individuals. Interpretations of these experiences often align with the person's cultural and religious background, yet the core elements remain remarkably consistent across different populations.

Research has shown that NDEs often lead to long-term effects, such as reduced fear of death, an increased sense of purpose, and a greater appreciation for life. Specific features of NDEs, like life reviews and encounters with mystical beings, are strongly associated with these transformative aftereffects.

A minority of near-death experiences (NDEs) are reported as distressing or hellish, with studies indicating that approximately 1-2% of NDEs fall into this category. These experiences often include extreme fear, emotional anguish, desolation, visions of demonic creatures, intense cold or heat, and tormenting sounds. Research has shown that the occurrence of distressing NDEs is not necessarily linked to a person's moral character or religious beliefs.

Some researchers have suggested that negative NDEs might be influenced by pre-existing psychological factors, such as anxiety, depression, unresolved trauma, guilt, fear-based worldviews, or rigid belief systems about the afterlife. However, even individuals who initially experience a hellish NDE often report a transformation or rescue.

The link between nihilistic or fearful attitudes towards life and negative NDEs is an area of ongoing research, with some studies suggesting that individuals with a more positive outlook on life and death tend to have more positive NDEs.

The subjective nature of NDEs and the limitations of studying them scientifically make it challenging to draw definitive conclusions. While there appears to be some correlation between pre-existing beliefs, attitudes, and the nature of NDEs, the relationship is complex and not fully understood, warranting further research.

I end this chapter with this section on NDEs as the stories by other people can work as a reminder of what is truly important in life.

> *You have a mission in life, and each human life has a purpose.*
>
> *Unconditional love is a fundamental force in the universe, and love and service to others are key to growth.*
>
> *Your appreciation for life increases, and values shift towards compassion and spiritual growth. Do not take life for granted.*
>
> *Fear of death diminishes or disappears after an NDE.*
>
> *You are part of a larger, interconnected consciousness. There is a sense of cosmic unity or oneness.*
>
> *The experience feels "more real than real," suggesting a different level of consciousness. The concept of linear time may not apply in the NDE state.*
>
> *NDEs often result in lasting positive changes to personality and behaviour, including increased authenticity and spirituality.*
>
> *Actions are judged by their intent and impact on others, not just the deeds themselves.*
>
> *Guidance and support are available from a higher source. Many report encountering spiritual beings or deceased loved ones.*
>
> *Your perception of reality changes reality, and this perception can influence the NDE experience itself.*

Afterword

It is done!

Writing this book has been a journey, much like the one it describes. Each section reflects years of exploration, experimentation, and occasional failure. It's not a polished manifesto, nor is it a definitive answer to life's questions. Instead, it's an attempt to map out ideas, provide tools for reflection, and challenge assumptions about reality, authenticity, and the role of Consciousness in shaping our experience.

After months of almost uninterrupted writing, fixing text, solving technical problems, creating illustrations, choosing colours, learning about ISBNs, self-publishing, and finding a print-on-demand service, I am finally here. There are many people I could mention by name who have helped me in one way or another. But I won't.

This book reflects countless conversations and interactions I've had over the years. Discussions often wandered into politics, biology, finance, and more, helping me understand the world, the people I spoke to, and, above all, myself. Each exchange—whether brief or in-depth—has contributed to shaping my thoughts and refining my ideas. Life is built on many interactions, not just a few. Rather than listing names, I've decided to focus on the ideas themselves. This approach aligns with the nature of this book, which is grounded in logic and personal exploration. To those, I've spoken with, know that your words, questions, and perspectives have played a part in this journey, even if not explicitly mentioned here.

Some people helped me with proofreading, and for that, I am deeply thankful. I've learned how difficult it is to proofread my texts. I get blind to what I've actually written and assume too much—what I meant to say, not what is on the page. So, thank you!

Then there are the protagonists and antagonists, the angels and demons in my life. By now, if you've read most of this book, you know I don't see these as opposites but as points on a spectrum, often closely connected. Without these forces—both helpful and hindering—I wouldn't be where I am now. I am a happy, blessed person. So, once again: thank you.

Afterword

This book isn't perfect, and neither is the journey it describes. Life, as I've written, is a game—not of winners and losers but of participation, growth, and alignment with your authentic Self. Mistakes are inevitable, and occasionally, they're necessary. They teach us what works and what doesn't, pushing us to refine our choices and move closer to what we might call low entropy—order, love, and understanding.

What's next? I already have ideas for what to write about next. Jacob Böhme interests me greatly; much of Tom's thinking resonates with his. Other topics on my mind include relationships, morality and ethics, and astrology. I might revisit the idea of a children's book version. Or I may take a break, return to painting, and focus on renovating the house. Time will tell. Whatever I choose, I intend to enjoy it.

As you close this book, I encourage you to reflect on what it means to live authentically. Not perfectly, not fearfully, but authentically. That means aligning your actions with the intentions of your Soul, even when it's difficult or unclear. It means recognising that growth isn't linear and that progress often looks like a series of small, imperfect steps.

This book ends here, but your journey doesn't. I dropped a few names, and you could use those to start your research. Take what resonates, leave what doesn't, and keep going. Keep trying, keep testing and measuring your progress.

The game isn't over yet.

www.ingramcontent.com/pod-product-compliance
Lightning Source LLC
Chambersburg PA
CBHW052019290426
44112CB00014B/2295